Language and Literacy Series

Dorothy S. Strickland, FOUNDING EDITOR
Celia Genishi and Donna E. Alvermann, SERIES EDITORS

ADVISORY BOARD: Richard Allington, Kathryn Au, Bernice Cullinan,
Colette Daiute, Anne Haas Dyson, Carole Edelsky, Janet Emig,
Shirley Brice Heath, Connie Juel, Susan Lytle, Timothy Shanahan

---

Volumes in the NCRLL Collection: Approaches to Language and Literacy Research

JoBeth Allen and Donna E. Alvermann, EDITORS

On Teacher Inquiry:
Approaches to Language and Literacy Research
Dixie Goswami, Ceci Lewis, Marty Rutherford, and Diane Waff

On Discourse Analysis in Classrooms:
Approaches to Language and Literacy Research
David Bloome, Stephanie Power Carter, Beth Morton Christian,
Samara Madrid, Sheila Otto, Nora Shuart-Faris, and Mandy Smith,
with contributions by Susan R. Goldman and Douglas Macbeth

On Critically Conscious Research:
Approaches to Language and Literacy Research
Arlette Ingram Willis, Mary Montavon, Helena Hall,
Catherine Hunter, LaTanya Burke, and Ana Herrera

On Ethnography:
Approaches to Language and Literacy Research
Shirley Brice Heath and Brian V. Street,
with Molly Mills

On Formative and Design Experiments:
Approaches to Language and Literacy Research
David Reinking and Barbara A. Bradley

On the Case:
Approaches to Language and Literacy Research
Anne Haas Dyson and Celia Genishi

On Qualitative Inquiry:
Approaches to Language and Literacy Research
George Kamberelis and Greg Dimitriadis

ON TEACHER INQUIRY

Approaches to Language and Literacy Research

(AN NCRLL VOLUME)

Dixie Goswami
Ceci Lewis
Marty Rutherford
Diane Waff

Teachers College
Columbia University
New York and London

NCRLL

National Conference
on Research in Language
and Literacy

Published by Teachers College Press, 1234 Amsterdam Avenue, New York, NY 10027

Published in association with the National Conference on Research in Language and Literacy (NCRLL). For more information about NCRLL, see http://www.ncrll.org.

Portions of Chapter 3 appeared in "Exploring Language, Identity, and the Power of Narrative" by Ceci Lewis, Michael Armstrong, Mary Guerrero, and Lusanda Mayikanna, and "Talking Proper" Say Sandwich, Not Sangwich," by Ceci Lewis, *Bread Loaf Teacher Network Magazine,* Spring 2002. Reprinted with permission.

Library of Congress Cataloging-in-Publication Data

On teacher inquiry : approaches to language and literacy research / Dixie Goswami [et al.].
    p. cm.—(Language and literacy series)
    Includes bibliographical references and index.
    ISBN 978-0-8077-4945-6 (pbk.)—ISBN 978-0-8077-4946-3 (hardcover)
  1. Action research in education. 2. Language arts—Research. I. Goswami, Dixie.
    LB1028.24.O5 2009
    428'.0072—dc22

                                                            2008043596

ISBN: 978-0-8077-4945-6 (paperback)
ISBN: 978-0-8077-4946-3 (hardcover)

Printed on acid-free paper
Manufactured in the United States of America

16 15 14 13 12 11 10 09   8 7 6 5 4 3 2 1

This book is dedicated to the great community of teachers who look to their students and their practice for knowledge and understanding and to the countless networks and affiliations that support and sustain them.

Contents

From the NCRLL Editors

If nothing is as practical as a good theory, no research approach may be as useful to the improvement of educational practice as engaging in teacher inquiry.

In this volume, Dixie Goswami, Ceci Lewis, Marty Rutherford, and Diane Waff invite us into their classrooms, schools, and teacher inquiry networks. They employ Janet Emig's inquiry paradigm, a powerful framework for educators researching their own practice. With this common framework and four distinctive voices, the authors share the rich intellectual tradition of teacher inquiry through their respective studies. Marty Rutherford examines the cultural and linguistic resources of middle school English language learners in Oakland California, as these science students formed a learning community steeped in talking, writing, and concept development. Ceci Lewis analyzes an online dialogue involving her Latino students with literacy educators and students from around the world about complex relationships between the language of the classroom and the language and culture of their Southwest community. Diane Waff explores how, as an African American educator in an urban district in the Northeast engaged in school reform, she participated in three inquiry groups investigating complex issues of race, ethnicity, social class, and linguistic diversity. Dixie Goswami, the Patron Saint of Teacher Research, weaves these accounts together with threads of history, politics, and passion.

We believe that this book, like others in the NCRLL collection, will be useful to a wide range of researchers. The authors do not offer a blueprint for "doing teacher research"; rather, they explicate an inquiry framework that provides a challenging yet stable scaffold for teachers, teacher educators, administrators, and other educators examining their practice. In addition to sharing their own research, the authors introduce readers to some of their "published friends" in a helpful annotated bibliography that includes examples of language and literacy research by teachers as well as references for conducting teacher inquiry, building theory, and finding institutional support.

On Teacher Inquiry is the seventh volume in the National Conference on Research in Language and Literacy (NCRLL) collection of books published by Teachers College Press. These volumes, written by some of the most prominent researchers in the field, offer insights, information, and guidance in understanding and employing various approaches to researching language and literacy. The first six highly acclaimed books are *On Qualitative Inquiry* by George Kamberelis and Greg Dimitriadis; *On the Case* by Anne Haas Dyson and Celia Genishi; *On Formative and Design Experiments* by David Reinking and Barbara Bradley; *On Ethnography* by Shirley Brice Heath and Brian Street with Molly Mills; *On Critically Conscious Research* by Arlette Willis, Helena Hall, Mary Montovan, Catherine Hunter, LaTanya Burke, and Ana Herrera; and *On Discourse Analysis in Classrooms* by David Bloome, Stephanie Power Carter, Beth Morton Christian, Samara Madrid, Sheila Otto, Nora Shuart-Faris, and Mandy Smith, with contributions by Susan Goldman and Douglas Macbeth. Subsequent books in this collection will include explorations of narrative inquiry by David Schaafsma and Ruth Vinz, mixed methods by Robert Calfee and Melanie Sperling, and quantitative research methods by P. David Pearson and Barbara Taylor.

The "On..." books: where language and literacy researchers turn to learn. Welcome to the conversation.

Acknowledgments

I want to acknowledge the support of the Bread Loaf School of English, my students and colleagues there, and the remarkable members of the Bread Loaf Teacher Network—young people and adults. Thanks also to the expert, generous help of Carolyn Benson, Judy Jessup, and Sandy LeGault with all aspects of this book.

—*Dixie Goswami*

My experience as a teacher-researcher could not have been possible without the assistance of many individuals. I would like to thank the Spencer Foundation for generously funding this project and for giving us the opportunity to explore the issue of language acquisition. A special thank you to my fellow researchers: Michael Armstrong, Mary Guerrero, Lusanda Mayikana, Khulekani Njokweni, Samuel Pacheco, Veronica Sanchez, Ntokozo Zulu, and the wonderful students from Lawrence, Katherine, Franyeliz, Jessica, Johanny, and Melvin. To the wise educators and researchers who helped guide our research: Courtney Cazden, Dixie Goswami, Marty Rutherford, and Steve Seidel. A very special thank you to my husband, De Lewis, whose support, love, and patience have provided me with great encouragement.

—*Ceci Lewis*

I want to thank every single teacher who looked at her students with careful eyes and understood that teaching is never teaching without learning. I want to thank every single student I ever had who taught me to pay attention to them as my primary teachers. I want to thank the Brookline Teacher Research group for showing me what it means to be a teacher who does research: You changed my life. There are not big enough words to express my gratitude for Dixie, Diane, Ceci and Tom McKenna who help me teach and think about teaching in more powerful ways every day. Sarah Rutherford listened to so many versions of my chapter, her listening was my greatest composition tool, and her wit my greatest delight. Finally and always I want to thank Dean Rutherford who is my inspiration, muse, critic and best friend.

—Marty Rutherford

I would like to thank colleagues from the Philadelphia Writing Project, The Bread Loaf Teacher Network, the Carnegie Academy for the Advancement of Teaching and Learning (CASTL), and the National Writing Project for their support of my work as a teacher researcher. I also wish to thank my colleague and friend, Susan Lytle, for introducing me to the field of teacher research and the power of inquiry to advance positive school change. For helpful suggestions and comments to early chapter drafts, I wish to thank Dixie Goswami, Emily Bartels, Susan Lytle and Marty Rutherford. Finally, I would like to express my deepest gratitude to Suzann Ordile for her valuable and productive collaboration on our teacher research project.

—Diane Waff

Finally, we all owe a profound debt to Janet Emig, for her wisdom and scholarship, her questions and challenges, and her belief that professionally and personally, teachers can be agents of change. We would also like to acknowledge our gratitude for the peer reviewers who carefully read and responded to our book: Cindy Ballenger, Bob Fecho, Karen Gallas, and Susan Lytle. We would also like to take this opportunity to thank JoBeth Allen, Donna Alvermann, and Meg Lemke, all of whom have patiently worked with us as we developed this text.

CHAPTER 1

"What's Going on Here?"

Seeking Answers Through Teacher Inquiry

DIXIE GOSWAMI
MARTY RUTHERFORD

Teacher research just isn't like other forms of research, in part because there is no blueprint for how to do it. Over the last 25 years it has also become clear that there is no single definition for what "it" is. That was the joy and the challenge of writing this book. The purpose of this book, therefore, is to put forth a framework, a set of examples, and some guidelines for designing and conducting inquiry projects in your own classrooms and schools—with your colleagues and your students.

When the seminal book *Reclaiming the Classroom: Teacher Research as an Agency for Change* was published in 1987, coeditors Dixie Goswami and Peter Stillman wrote in the preface about the habit of inquiry that had always been at the heart of good teaching, about the scholarly traditions that inform teacher inquiries, and about the potential of collaborative inquiries to help us create communities of learners within classrooms and beyond. The book was groundbreaking in that the contributors included outstanding K–12 teachers who had not published before and others whose scholarship on language and learning had inspired and informed what was called an "alternative research tradition." *Reclaiming* set forth no presecribed strategies for teacher research, but rather emphasized the rich diversity of motives, methods, and cultural resources that all contributors brought to the conversation.

While it is true that there is no blueprint, there are, in fact, shared characteristics held in common by teacher research and other research methods. When engaging in teacher research, the challenge becomes choosing among different methodologies to find the one that best serves the specific context and particulars—hence the need for an inquiry paradigm. For this book we turned to Janet Emig, whose now classic comprehensive and rigorous framework helps us to conceptualize teacher inquiry in ways that might be useful to teachers who are considering diving in. A collection of Emig's essays was published in 1983 as *The Web of Meaning*, and we will be citing it throughout our book.

In this chapter we want, first, to talk about the value added from teacher research and, second, to unpack Emig's inquiry paradigm and demonstrate how it is an important first step when engaging in systematic research about teaching and learning.

WHY DO TEACHER RESEARCH?

For teachers who are contemplating adding teacher research to their repertoire of practices, the most important consideration centers on the value added from such endeavors—specifically, why do teacher research? The simple answer is that teacher research is needed. The kind of wisdom and knowledge that is generated from what Cochran-Smith and Lytle (1993) call "looking from the inside out" is not reproducible through other kinds of research paradigms. As teachers, we are privileged participants in the world of teaching and learning of our students. Because of this position, the most essential thing we share is the need to know—to know if what we are teaching is serving the students under our care. Are they learning—learning to read, write, think, imagine, invent, and create? In this era of abundant assessment, we know a lot about scores on tests, rankings, and percentiles; but all too often, too many of us are left not knowing if the students we teach are receiving enough of what they need to be great citizens, strong and productive members of the communities they inhabit who are able to make a decent living because they can think, write, and analyze their world. At the end of the day as teachers, we are often left wondering: Are we doing enough? How do we know? These are the essential questions that occupy the minds and hearts of so many of us when we walk into our classrooms. This is the reason to do teacher research: to document student learning—the kind of documentation that leads to answers to these essential questions.

What is teacher research good for? To answer this question, we return to *Reclaiming the Classroom* (Goswami & Stillman, 1987). Although there have been many fine things written about teacher research since then, almost all of them restate what was written in the preface to that book. We take the liberty of paraphrasing that list of reasons to emphasize the value added when teachers engage in research. Here is the revised list:

- Our teaching is transformed in important ways because we become theorists who articulate our intentions, test assumptions, and find connections with practice.
- We are transformed as teachers and writers by using many resources, many of our own making.
- We form networks: We work with others, learn from others, share with others.
- We become activists for young people and for our profession.
- Because we observe closely the young people under our care over long periods of time, we have special, privileged insights and knowledge.
- We know our students and classrooms in ways that others cannot. Yet others (parents, community members, administrators, policy makers, academics) urgently need the knowledge and information we generate.
- We are critical, responsive readers and users of current research and curriculum. We are less apt to thoughtlessly accept others' theories, other people's ways of teaching our youth. Our authority is more systematically grounded in practice, and as a result, we are more cautious in our assessment of curricula, methods, and materials.
- Our research does not cost large sums of money.
- While a single study done by one teacher doing research is not definitive, taken together our studies about teaching and learning provide insights and understandings outside what is produced by specialists and external evaluators.
- We collaborate with our students to answer questions important to both teachers and students, drawing on community resources in new and important ways.

- The nature of classroom discourse and learning changes
  when inquiry begins. When students work with us
  (their teachers) to answer real questions, an intrinsic
  motivation for talking, reading, thinking, writing, and
  learning is created.

These are the reasons for teacher research. In becoming teachers who carefully and systematically document our practice, simply put, we do better. We are better prepared to understand the very particular needs of our students, the effectiveness of our teaching, and the process of student learning. To borrow from Michael Armstrong's (2006) work, through the careful observing of children we learn firsthand, up close and personal, about the special qualities, needs, and challenges facing the students that populate our classrooms. The need to engage in this work is nothing short of essential. Finding a way to accomplish this work within the fast-paced life of teaching is a challenge that this book will help teachers meet.

Emig's Inquiry Paradigm

We noted above that unlike other forms of research, there is no specific method associated with teacher research. As practitioners interested in knowing more about the intersection between teaching and learning in our classrooms, we draw from a variety of other traditions such as qualitative research, case study, ethnography, and so on. This flexibility in choosing a particular way of looking is at once the strength of this kind of work and a challenge.

It is not new information that classrooms are complex, layered communities that are beehives of activity in every single moment. Interactions, thoughts, cultures, and subcultures coexist simultaneously, making documentation of anything, at the very least, a challenge. Thus we need methods of conducting research that are flexible and easily adapted to the complexity of doing research in our own classrooms, on our students and practice. However, adapting and changing methods of any kind is a slippery slope. Methods cannot be changed because of a whim or particular context. There should be some kind of overarching logic that helps determine why one choice of shaping an inquiry makes more sense than another.

As teachers interested in documenting learning for ourselves and others, we wanted a way to give form and function to the internal and external questioning of our specific reasons for engaging in research. We needed more than directions for doing the research; we needed to construct new and rigorous ways to identify what ought to be examined and scrutinized. We needed guidelines for creating the kind of inquiry that would let us see behind the veil of the hustle and bustle of our classrooms and into the real world of how young people learn. This "something" we were looking for was more than a research method particular to an individual research project. We sought some mechanism or structure that would guide our thinking, looking, and understanding, that would help us plan, implement, and analyze our research. We needed a framework.

Our search ended with the discovery/recovery of Janet Emig's essay "Inquiry Paradigms and Writing," first published in 1981 and included in the collection we mentioned earlier. Emig raises essential questions about literacy research:

> What in the universe constitutes evidence? And how do we perceive/select, gather/arrange, value/judge entities and processes to fulfill our definitions? Our responses concerning the nature, organization, and evaluation of evidence reveal our inquiry paradigms, both those we elect to inhabit, and those we may even help to create. (Emig, 1983, p. 159)

To begin the unpacking of the meaning and usefulness of Emig's paradigm, it is important to understand her thinking. Early in the essay she explained why she used the words *inquiry paradigm*. Like so much of Emig's work, each word carried powerful meaning intentionally chosen to enhance the usefulness of the tool.

According to Emig, in order to understand teaching and learning in the classroom setting, the term *inquiry* is more useful than the term *research*. Inquiry has greater breadth for addressing context and connected issues. Emig borrows from Thomas Kuhn (1970) when unpacking the meaning of *paradigm*. Kuhn defines *paradigm* as an explanatory matrix. In this case, *explanatory* means giving reasons or details that help to understand something. *Matrix* is a situation or circumstance that allows or encourages the origin, development, or growth of something. Taken together, these words imply understanding something within a particular context where growth or development takes place. Or as Emig (1983) says, "An inquiry paradigm then is the explanatory matrix for any systematic investigation of phenomena" (p. 159). This particular inquiry paradigm served the four authors of this book as an essential first step and accompanying tool to frame our understanding of the phenomena in each of our classrooms and inquiry communities. The straightforward design of this inquiry paradigm created a systematic approach for looking at our classrooms and our learning communities with new eyes. This allowed us, as Clifford Geertz (1986) suggests, to make the familiar strange—strange enough so that we can find new understanding and clarity about teaching and learning.

According to Emig, to qualify as an inquiry paradigm, an endeavor must be informed by six distinct characteristics:

- A *governing gaze*—how and why do we see and perceive what we see?
- An acknowledged, or at least conscious, set of *assumptions*—the things we believe to be true.
- A *coherent theory* or theories—in other words, the strong reasons, hopefully based on good research, that inform our practice.
- An allegiance to an explicit or at least a tacit *intellectual tradition* that asks us to consider, to borrow from Jackie Royster (2000), "Whose company are we keeping?"
- An adequate *methodology*—how you actually conduct your research in your class.
- An *indigenous logic* consonant with all of the above.

What follows is an explanation about the practical applications of each of these six elements.

Governing Gaze

Prior to beginning any kind of inquiry it is important to identify what is "governing our gaze." Emig (1983) describes it this way:

We see what we elect to see. We have, as the metaphor puts it, a gaze that is governed by our expectations, which in turn are governed by our experiences and what we have decided cognitively to make of them: by, that is, our hypotheses . . . , schemes . . . , and constructs . . . . (p. 160)

Acknowledging that we have a governing gaze leads to an essential set of questions, for example, What influences the way we view our students? Their capacity to learn? Their use of language—first and second? Understanding the things that govern our gaze allows for positioning ourselves in relation to the research we are doing. Everything about governing gaze is specific to a certain time, place, and context, as well as to our identities and personal histories. A different time and circumstance would alter the gaze because we would be looking at different students, learning in different ways.

Assumptions

For Emig, it is impossible for anyone to proceed with any inquiry without explicitly identifying a set of assumptions. Assumptions create the parameters of the inquiry. Whether looking at how one learns to write, discuss science, or read for understanding, the set of assumptions that frame the inquiry creates boundaries that can contain the inquiry. Otherwise, an inquiry can run the risk of becoming unruly and unfocused. Creating a clear set of assumptions allows for more clarity.

Emig (1983) uses the example of conducting an inquiry into the nature of writing to explain what she means. In so doing, she articulates a set of things that an inquiry into the nature of learning to write would "inescapably concern" (p. 164). She then unpacks the elements of her assumptions. For example, one assumption is that any inquiry into writing would involve looking at student writing. But what does looking at student writing mean? Looking at one sample or several samples taken over time? How is a particular inquiry impacted when there are too few samples to document change over time? What happens when writing samples are collected in a way that is not representative of the way students write?

Assumptions about what should be in place in order to have a rich and informative inquiry are essential. The specific articulation and unpacking of these assumptions leads the researcher to gain more and more clarity about how the inquiry needs to be framed and conducted.

Coherent Theory

Each inquiry needs to be built upon a single theory or set of theories. Human beings are theorizers. We act on what we think is best. As teachers, theorizing is a minute-by-minute enterprise. We teach a particular child how to read in a particular way because we believe that it will best serve the student's need, based on our beliefs about how children become literate. Thinking of theorizing in this way led Emig to explain that the role of coherent theories in conducting any inquiry can be likened to a set of coherent and explicit beliefs. For example, believing that knowledge is socially constructed would lead to an inquiry that involves students working together to learn something. The theory leads to and follows upon the way we organize an episode for learning. Systematic inquiry allows us to see the usefulness of the theory. The explicitness of articulating the theory makes it available for scrutiny. Again Emig (1983) calls on friends to help her articulate big ideas, in this case Jerome Bruner: "A theory is also a way of stating tersely what one already knows without the burden of detail. In this sense it is a canny and economical way of keeping in mind a vast amount while thinking about very little" (quoted in Emig, p. 15). The usefulness of theory is in the explicit understanding how it is helpful to the practice of teaching and learning. Because the implementation of theories in the classroom has such powerful implications, close scrutiny and deep understanding of their impact is nothing short of essential.

Intellectual Tradition

Taken together, our governing gaze, our particular assumptions, and our theories form a set of guidelines for finding existing research that contributes to the new inquiry that will be undertaken. The purpose of this part of the framework is to closely examine and explicitly articulate the relationship between others' work and our own, and to understand the influence that work has on our practice. As Emig (1983) most elegantly asks, "Whom then do we seek and cite as ancestors and authorities?" (p. 166). Once we find and name what we consider to be wisdom, then we can recognize and evaluate the value added.

Another layer of importance that is particular to teacher research is that we begin to incorporate and build upon other teachers' work. It is essential that we add to the intellectual tradition. In *Reclaiming the Classroom*, Goswami and Stillman (1986) pointed out that one teacher's inquiry is perhaps most beneficial to his or her own classroom. But several inquiries, by different teachers on the same topic and in varied contexts taken together, serve as powerful knowledge to inform the practices of others. Referring to and using other people's research as support for our new inquiries builds a powerful "web of meaning" for our own practice and others (Emig, 1983, p. v).

Methodology

Every part of the paradigm that has been articulated up to this point contributes to the design of the methodology. Only after careful consideration of each of the pieces in relation to the specific topic of the inquiry in the particular setting, at the exact moment, with an identified student or group of students can one decide on a method for examination of the phenomenon. This is where drawing on the work of others is so important. A graphic artist friend once described his work as "cheat art." What he meant by this term is that there is little new under the sun—there are simply many new ways of organizing existing ideas. This is the central idea here. There are many fine methods that exist. We will name some in the final chapter. It is left to each individual researcher at the moment of designing the inquiry to decide which one is the best fit. For example, would a case study best inform in this context? An ethnography? What kind of data is best at the start of the project? During the project? After the project? It is impossible to answer these questions in the abstract. Time, circumstance, and context are the best indicators on how to proceed—that and reading, finding, and listening to fine examples of others people's work. This book offers three examples in Chapters 2, 3, and 4 and points the way to many others in Chapter 5.

Indigenous Logic

Simply put, indigenous logic means that once all the pieces of this paradigm are examined from the perspective of the inquiry, you ask yourself:

- Does this make sense?
- Is it worth it?
- Is there something to be learned here?
- Does the careful articulation of my governing gaze, assumptions, theories, and ideas; the position of others in my intellectual traditions; and my ensuing methodology create that foundation for systematic inquiry?

These are essential questions before beginning any inquiry. Each particular context begets a certain set of assumptions, which in turn leads to the assembling of a very specific set of theories—which in turn is the foundation for initiating specific ways of looking, methods for collecting data, making sense out of, and learning from what was observed.

Inquiry into practice—deep understanding of the ways of teaching and learning—is the most significant contribution each of us can make to the students under our care and others in this profession. Teacher research—systematic, carefully conceived, and well-executed inquiries—are urgently needed in this time of excessive testing that does not even begin to document learning. However, Emig (1983) cautions:

> What is the value in making this elaborate—some might say over-elaborate—characterization of inquiry paradigms . . . ? First, it is quite possible that unexamined inquiries are not worth making. Two, it is equally possible that impoverished or immature inquiries are also not worth making and the surest way to identify these is to set them against mature paradigms and fully realized inquiries. (p. 168)

OVERVIEW OF THIS BOOK

Although there is no blueprint for teacher research, there is a rich intellectual tradition. This book aims to provide a taste of that tradition and a way forward for more teachers to contribute to the abundance of the rich knowledge that teachers and their students produce through rigorous and systematic inquiry. The following three chapters are examples of teacher research carried out by Marty Rutherford, Ceci Lewis, and Diane Waff. Although their inquiries were done with other partners at widely separated times and places, they demonstrate the power of Emig's paradigm because they are bound together by this framework.

Our reasons for turning to Emig do not have to do only with theories, research traditions, and methodologies, for she spoke most urgently about the politics of teaching and learning, in terms that we understand. In "Literacy and Freedom," her keynote address to the 1982 Conference on College Composition and Communication, Emig called on members of the profession, in terms that still ring true today, to insist on the relationships among writing, educating the imagination, and survival: "We, and our view of literacy are needed—they are the only ones I know subtle, humane, and tough enough for these times. May our beliefs prevail; and may we and our students, like our earth itself, survive and prosper" (Emig, 1983, p. 178). The narratives Marty, Ceci, and Diane have written are needed: they are subtle, humane, and tough enough for these times. Throughout his long career, James Britton claimed that a good story is a powerful argument. These good stories are powerful arguments for "cultures of collaboration."

The four authors of this book have a number of shared affiliations and networks that overlap, as well as discourse communities (local and otherwise) that are separate and wildly diverse. Yet we are all members of the Bread Loaf Teacher Network, a "blended" professional learning community that allows us to collaborate personally and electronically. In that spirit of collaboration, Dixie will introduce each of the next three chapters to help create the "web of meaning" we seek to offer with this book. Following the stories of teacher inquiry, the concluding chapter provides an annotated bibliography of some useful and generative work that has assisted all of us, at one time or another.

CHAPTER 2

FOSTERING COMMUNITIES OF LANGUAGE LEARNERS

And While We Are at It— Writers, Readers, Speakers, and Thinkers!

MARTY RUTHERFORD

DIXIE GOSWAMI: *Marty Rutherford was an experienced, savvy teacher in Oakland when she concluded that her assumptions about her children's lives and the cultural and linguistic resources they brought to her classroom were, in fact, based on her own life and circumstances. The story Marty tells is about becoming part of a middle school science and literacy program and her "conversion experience," in Emig's terminology (1983, p. 141). Working with her coteacher in this program, Marty carried out case studies of four students. Marty's account of her own inquiry reveals that she was part of overlapping communities of learners with students at the center.*

Marty and her coteachers were engaged in their separate inquiries and at the same time talking and writing to each other about their observations and experiences. Ann Brown and Joseph Campione, as well as Jerome Bruner, Annemarie Palincsar, and others, visited their classrooms, gathered and analyzed data, and talked and wrote with Marty and her coteachers. Before her research project ended, Marty had been thoroughly immersed in theories about how learning communities rich with talk and writing foster language acquisition and cognitive development.

Marty wondered at the outset if the close observation of four children would give her knowledge and insights about other chil-

dren; before her study ended her inquiry paradigm had shifted. Two aspects of Marty's inquiry are especially important: (1) her active participation in several discourse communities simultaneously (her classroom and the classroom community—parents and school, her coteachers and coresearchers, the larger circle of researchers who found meaning in her teaching); and (2) what she did and what she said and wrote.

Read Marty's chapter as an open-ended narrative that takes us from a classroom in Oakland where she had questions about herself as a teacher and her students as learners, to participation in a highly visible school-reform program, to a point where membership in learning communities that include inquiries about literacy are part of her professional—and personal—life. It is just such questions that lead teachers to become researchers in their own classrooms, researching on both the macrolevel (school reform) and the microlevel (how is it affecting my students).

But also read Marty's chapter as a case for affiliations and networks facilitated by technology that foster communities of inquiry. Not all teachers have opportunities to collaborate with teachers in their own schools; not all classrooms will be living laboratories for distinguished scholars. Yet technology provides the potential for pooling collective knowledge and collaborative problem solving in the networks and affiliations that are increasingly available to all teachers and their students. We must now think of Marty's participation in various learning communities and of the numerous, powerful teacher research networks available in this digital age.

In the last 2 decades, the literacy demands in the American workforce have increased dramatically. Economists and educators agree that mastery of basic skills is not enough (Cazden, 1999; Murnane & Levy, 1996; Valdés, 1998; 2001). Students of the twenty-first century must have the ability to communicate effectively both orally and in writing. Today's teachers are expected to build classrooms that foster these "new literacies," which require not only the ability to read and write complex texts on paper, but also to communicate in multilayered rhetorical contexts on the Internet and in the other technology-mediated formats that pervade contemporary life. Taken together, these reasons created the framework for my inquiry. When I conducted this research, I was a teacher in a sixth-grade urban classroom. Well over half of my students were bilingual. There were nine different languages represented in my student population. My research was urgent. I needed to understand if the way teaching and learning was organized in my classroom was serving to help all of the students acquire the aforementioned new literacies.

It is perhaps a universal characteristic of teacher research that the motivation to do it in the first place comes from a great passion and a desire to examine and reflect on one's own teaching in order to improve. In doing teacher research, one takes a personal inventory of one's classroom and the practices enacted there. Like other teachers doing research on their practice, I had questions about my students' response to my teaching:

- What do these young people need to know?
- What do they want to know?
- How do they understand what I teach?
- Are they learning to write?
- How can I be sure?

Such questions are always on my mind. To find the answers to these, and perhaps even more, questions, I turned to teacher research.

In this chapter, I describe my process of doing teacher research. Like most teacher researchers, and certainly those represented in this book, my primary purpose was to improve my practice. Second, I hoped to build useable knowledge. The need to know more set in motion a daunting task: to conduct a systematic, in-depth inquiry into the teaching and learning in my classroom. In composing and conducting my research, I was humbled by the enormity of the endeavor.

For all of us—Ceci Lewis (Chapter 3), Diane Waff (Chapter 4), and I—the research process was multilayered, intentionally planned and executed, yet very different in content and contexts. We began by making explicit to ourselves and others what shaped our vision, our "governing gaze" according to Emig. Next, in various ways, we each built our knowledge about the subject of our investigations in order to clarify our assumptions and build a theoretical frame. The theoretical frame facilitated the design and shape of our research. A slow "walk" through my process, followed by a summary of my own teacher research will help illuminate these ideas.

WHAT GOVERNED MY GAZE?

The way I see or understand teaching and learning was deeply influenced by three important experiences:

1. I had a conversation with a student that changed my way of seeing the world.
2. I was introduced to teacher research and realized that teachers have a responsibility for building knowledge and understanding about classroom practices and the way students learn.
3. I was part of a whole-school change effort.

Seeing My Students Differently.

While conducting this research, I was teaching in an urban school that housed students and teachers from many cultures and language groups. On average, each classroom was populated by 32 to 34 students speaking anywhere from five to nine different home languages such as Mandarin, Spanish, Cambodian, Vietnamese, Samoan, and Tongan. In a myriad of ways, the majority of my students came from circumstances very different from my own White, middle-class, monolingual upbringing. A small story best explains the difference. One Monday morning, a student in my class, Alzonia, asked me how my weekend went. "Not so hot—we got robbed," I replied.

"Oh, what a coincidence!" Alzonia responded. "We got robbed too. What did they steal?"

I told her the robbers took a bunch of little things, nothing of consequence. Alzonia expressed mild sympathy and explained that "her" robbers stole the family's Uzi. Quite taken aback, I asked if this might not have been a good thing—to which she calmly replied, "Marty, you will never understand my life." Of course she was right.

The bigger point here is not that I experienced a shocking exchange with a student, one that clearly illustrated the difference between my life and hers. Indeed I was well versed in and sensitive to issues facing linguistic minority students, having spent many years teaching inner-city classrooms full of students with very different home languages and life experiences. Until that moment, however, what governed my gaze was *my* life experience. This moment was a fundamental turning point for me. It forced me to recognize that all I knew and understood about how students learn was only useful if I altered my gaze so that I saw their needs through *their* lived experiences and cultural perspectives, not mine.

It is not uncommon for teachers to have these kinds of transitional moments; the gold is when we see the impact for our teaching (Fecho, 2004; Obidah & Teel, 2001). This was my moment. In Chapters 3 and 4 my coauthors tell of their moments. As you read, think about these transformative moments, and ask yourself, "What governs my gaze?"

Recognizing Teachers as Knowledge Makers

In the late 1980s I learned about teacher research. This was an extraordinary experience for me. Prior to that time I thought of myself, and teachers in general, as consumers of knowledge. I was invited to one of the first small conferences put on by the Brookline Teacher Research Seminar (BTRS, 2003). Teachers from an elementary school in Brookline, Massachusetts, were exploring the role of talk and learning in each of their classrooms. Although the notion of closely observing children was completely new to me, I soon learned that it was a well-established practice, if not yet represented in published work (Armstrong, 2006; Branscombe, Goswami, & Schwartz, 1992; BTRS, 2003; Cochran-Smith & Lytle, 1993; Goswami & Stillman, 1987; Himley & Carini, 2000). I was awed and inspired by the way the teachers in the Brookline Seminar collected observations about their students and then proceeded to make sense out of these everyday events in the company of their peers. Their sense-making process brought forward a new kind of knowledge, knowledge born from watching, reflecting, and sharing (Cochran-Smith & Lytle, 1993; Himley & Carini, 2000; Waff, this volume).

Working with the Brookline Teacher Research Seminar led to two life-altering actions: I established a teacher researcher group at my school, and I enrolled in a nearby graduate school program so that I could learn more about literacy and language acquisition. Closely watching the students under my care was not only illuminating in terms of understanding how they learned and what they needed, it also exposed my own inadequacies as a teacher. As a result, I needed to know more. Finding out that there was such a thing as teacher research altered my gaze. I realized that systematic research on my own practice impacted the way I operated in the classroom—it made it better. In so doing I began to build a special kind of knowledge that can only come from the inside out (Cochran-Smith & Lytle, 1993).

Changing Our School

As with other authors in this book, my work as a teacher researcher was deeply influenced by my colleagues. The inquiry described in this chapter took place while I was involved in designing and building a curriculum called Fostering a Community of Learners (FCL). More will be said about the substance of the curriculum later, but suffice it to say that participation in the FCL project changed virtually every aspect of our teaching from content to process. This radical change process made it essential to have some form of systematic documentation as a mechanism for recording and reflecting upon what worked and what did not. As a group we decided that each teacher would look closely at one aspect of our shared work. My coteacher Doris Ash (1995) chose to look at the content; another teacher, Jill Walker (1998), was concerned about how the small groups functioned. I was interested in the developing literacy practices of my linguistic minority students (Rutherford, 1995). We were deeply dependent on our own and each other's research in order to understand the impact of the changes we were making in our classrooms and practice. Our research informed our practice, and reciprocally our practice informed the way the classrooms functioned. The need for clarity about our teaching and learning was immediate and urgent because it directly affected our students. Our collective emerging awareness of the power of teacher research made it imperative that we take responsibility for documenting that work. We believed that our insider perspective would be important not only for informing others about our work but, more immediately, for deepening our understanding of the way linguistic minority students learn to speak, write, think, imagine, invent, and create in a language that is not their mother tongue.

In my experience, as well as that of my coauthors in this book (see Chapters 3 and 4), the professional, collaborative relationships of colleagues was an essential component of the research and the method of doing research. Colleagues and coresearchers served as important resources for thinking through research designs, gathering data, analyzing findings, and incorporating the new knowledge into practice. As you think about your own research, consider the circumstances surrounding your inquiry, and ask yourself questions such as the following:

- How can my colleagues enhance and inform my work?
- What kind of group might facilitate my research?
- What ideas can be drawn from our experiences?
- What needs to be changed to fit my unique and particular contexts?

LEARNING FROM OTHERS, BUILDING ASSUMPTIONS, INTEGRATING THEORIES

The most significant pre-teacher-inquiry activity for me was the careful articulation of what informed my practice and learning in my classroom in order to build my own theoretical framework to guide and inform my practice. Whether it is articulated or tacit, most teachers have a theoretical framework that is connected to a set of assumptions that inform their actions. Theorizing about practice happens every time we think in terms of cause and effect—if I do X, then Y is likely to happen. That process of if-then speculation is theorizing. The difference between having a theoretical framework and using it to inform decision making about teaching and learning is making the framework explicit and available. In order to understand the framework I used for this particular inquiry, it is useful to look at my research question. Given the number of bilingual students that were struggling with the acquisition of advanced literacy skills, I was interested in knowing the answer to this question:

> In what ways did the delivery of content in multiple, interconnected, language-rich activities create the conditions for language learners to acquire school English— specifically, the ability to read, write, speak, and think?

This question created the parameters for building the theoretical framework that I needed in order to develop the appropriate lens through which I could compare and contrast the ways my students did or did not acquire the level of English they needed in order to be successful in school.

No one theory served to build my understanding about what it takes to create a great learning environment for bilingual students. Rather, as Jackie Royster (2000) suggests, "keeping company" with many experts on this topic allowed me to more deeply understand literacy acquisition issues facing English language learners. To build my own expertise in this area I read the work of many. My reading included work by school- and university-based researchers. Some of those resources are available in the last chapter of this book. An important benefit of teacher research is the value of learning from others in the service and thus gaining deeper understanding of our own contexts.

Three main theories guided my practice and the eventual analysis of the research presented in this chapter:

1. *Knowledge is socially constructed.* Experience and study taught me that knowledge is socially constructed (Vygotsky, 1978). Therefore, if I believe that gaining knowledge is a social endeavor, then my classroom needs to be organized so that students have a chance to talk to each other.

2. *Language acquisition requires many ways to talk and exchange ideas.* For many bilingual students, the classroom is the primary source for acquiring the target language (Mohan, 1986). Under the proper circumstances, the speech of the teacher and fellow students can serve two purposes: to convey subject matter and to supply comprehensive input for the learner (Swain, 1985). First, however, the teacher must organize the classroom culture so it accommodates talk and communication (Rutherford, 1995).

3. *The curriculum must be challenging, engaging, and generative.* Holistic activities based on unified concepts (as opposed to bits and pieces of knowledge) create a more coherent structure for all students, but especially for English language learners. The acquisition of higher level thinking and communication skills (reading, writing, listening, and speaking) is more expedient when taught in the service of a larger task such as writing a research paper.

Using these three theories about the nature of learning, the ways that students acquire English in school, and the role of a challenging curriculum, I had a way to seriously examine my own practice and the learning conditions in my classroom because they allowed for specific questioning. For example, when I looked at the data I collected about the input needs of a language learner, because I made this theory explicit, I could look at the quality of talk in my classroom and ask, "Is this the kind of talk that is comprehensible to the language learner?"

My theoretical framework informs my practice and my research. It tells me to organize my classroom, to foster talk, have interesting and engaging things for the students to learn, and to plan very specific ways for them to talk to each other. In terms of my research, it gives me a frame for my inquiry that is informed by theory. If I think students need to talk to learn, then what kinds of opportunities are there for them to talk to each other? Are they the right opportunities? The theory and the inquiry form a system of interconnected parts that can mutually inform each other when they are available for reflection.

Each new piece of research requires an altering of the theoretical framework. Certain theories may carry over, like the notion that knowledge is socially constructed, but every piece of research has its own nuances. As you prepare for your own research, ask yourself these questions: What theories inform my research? How will this theoretical frame guide my research?

ACKNOWLEDGING ASSUMPTIONS

Informed by experience and studies about second language learning and learning in general, I understood that classroom organization, interaction possibilities, and challenging content provide students with much needed opportunities to learn enough English so that they can participate fully in classroom learning. Opportunities to engage in serious, in-depth conversations in school-based content areas lead to and follow upon the acquisition of English (Ash, 1993; Brown, 1994; Rutherford, 1995). Moreover, I assumed that learning to communicate with peers in English was not enough for language learners to be successful in school. Successful participation in school requires bilingual students to read and understand age-appropriate texts and to communicate complex ideas in text and in speech in English. Language learners need ample support and timely feedback about the degree to which their comprehension and communicative skills are improving.

The purpose of my research was to see if my assumptions had merit. That is why my research question focused on understanding the intersection between teaching, learning, classroom organization, and the curriculum.

The clarity and specificity of my assumptions allowed for the development of clear and precise questions, which in turn shaped my research. Like Ceci Lewis (see Chapter 3), I was interested in issues facing bilingual students. But my focus was very different. I was interested in understanding how what I taught and the way I organized my classroom impacted the reading, writing, and speaking skills of four bilingual students. Ceci was interested in understanding what it meant to be bilingual. And while the overarching issue was the same, the focus was different, and that meant that the research itself was shaped on different considerations. Our different perspectives, research questions, and underlying theories and assumptions impacted the shape and content of our research. Though much more will be said about this shortly, consider how your particular gaze, assumptions, and theories inform and shape your research. Ask yourself the following questions:

- How might what I want to accomplish be different from other research?
- How might it be the same?
- What is it that I am trying to understand?
- Whose company might help me get a deeper understanding of the main issues?
- Whose work might help me shape my own research questions?

METHODS FOR CONDUCTING RESEARCH: HOW DID I LEARN WHAT I NEEDED TO KNOW?

The teacher research tradition in which I operated does not prescribe particular methods, but does provide multiple examples of methodologies teachers have used. Picking a method for conducting a piece of research is where the word *systematic* really becomes important. My research questions and what I want to know—taken together with my assumptions, theories, and governing gaze–determine what method of research will give me the most comprehensive information. Practically speaking, I designed my method of inquiry by unpacking each and every element of my question and created my ways of looking because of my understanding of my theories and assumptions. The importance of careful articulation of these aspects is essential to framing any well-executed, systematic inquiry.

In my case, I wanted to know *how* my students acquired English in the school setting. More specifically, I wanted to know how they did or did not become competent readers, writers, speakers, and thinkers in English. Because I was interested in the *how* of their learning, looking at test scores or any other work they produced without seeing them in the process of producing it would not enlighten me as to how they were or were not learning the amount of English they needed to learn in order to be successful in school. To answer my questions I needed to watch and listen to my students when they were engaged in the act of learning in order to gain a deeper understanding of their particular processes. To accomplish this goal, I needed to see them in their natural setting—in this case the classroom—interacting with their peers and with the curriculum (Bogdan & Biklen, 1982; Dyson & Genishi, 2004).

My method for this inquiry was what Dyson and Genishi (2004) call "making a case." I was interested in understanding something about how bilingual students acquire school English. Looking at more than one language learner in the particular setting of my classroom created the context for comparing and contrasting experiences beyond one example and enabled me to decide how what I learned should impact my practice. Though I will say more about how I chose the students later, it is important to know that I chose students who were at different levels in their capacity to read, write, speak, and think in "school English"—meaning the kind of academic language that is valued in classroom settings.

To engage in your own research, you will have to decide what to look at, how many students to study, and under what conditions when selecting what kind of method you will use. Notice the kinds of choices the other authors in this volume made. Both Ceci in Chapter 3 and Diane in Chapter 4 had very different research questions and very different contexts; thus their methods were different. It cannot be said too often that there is no one-size-fits-all in teacher research.

Collecting Data: The Where, Why, When and What

Because I wanted to see *how* my bilingual students were learning to communicate and comprehend talk and produce text in English, my data needed to include live examples of my focal students actually doing these things. Therefore, my "data collection site" was wherever and whenever they were actively engaged in reading, writing, thinking, and speaking.

In my classroom there were participant structures for each key activity, and by extension each key moment I needed to capture in my quest to understand my focal students' learning processes. For example, there were specified participant structures where students anticipated learning new material as a whole class, times set aside specifically to talk to peers about their evolving research and times to write and revise their research papers. Knowing what was expected during these predetermined times, called rotations, allowed the students to ready themselves for the work, especially the English language learners. Figure 2.1 explains the participant structures that made up the fabric of the day in my classroom.

Because my interest was in understanding how my students learned English in the school setting, the participant structures were golden opportunities to see up close and personal their language acquisition process. If I were interested in learning about how students developed slang, I would have observed them in another setting, for example, out on the playground. What I wanted to know determined where and when I collected data. Each teacher engaging in research faces the same challenge; thus it is essential to consider what particular activities need to be closely observed in order to understand how students are learning.

I was also interested in understanding the connection between talk, text production, and the acquisition of writing skills, so I observed my focal students during all phases of producing a group research paper. Understanding something about how my students were learning to write in English meant that I not only needed to collect samples of their writing, but I needed to take notes on them as I observed them in the process. Figure 2.2 delineates the process of writing the research paper. The paper took approximately 5 to 6 weeks to write and could best be described

Figure 2.1. Classroom Rotations

Participant Structure	Purpose	Frequency
Benchmark lesson	Whole-class activity: important content or process ideas discussed	As needed, approximately every 2 weeks
Cross talk	Whole-class activity where students present their emerging research ideas	As needed, approximately once a week
Research rotations	Class in 3 sections: 2 groups—research; 2 groups—reciprocal teaching; 2 groups—computer use	Everyday when there was not a benchmark, cross talk, or jigsaw
Jigsaw	Students in reconfigured groups to teach content of their work	At the end of every research cycle

as a kind of evolutionary process that happened in phases.

My students did all of their writing on computers. This greatly simplified the data collection process. I periodically downloaded all of the writing of my focal students so that I could have a paper copy. Students were required to date every document each day they wrote. "Save As" was my mantra: This meant when they opened up a document, they pressed "save as" and entered the day's date. In this way I had every version of every piece my students wrote. My students were very intrigued by the idea that I was doing research on them, so they were happy to help. In this regard they were coresearchers, though less formal, than the students in Ceci's research (see Chapter 3). There is tremendous power in engaging in research with your students; insights into learning and teaching increase exponentially. Finally, because I was interested in the connection between talk and text produc-

Figure 2.2 Phases of Writing the Group Research Paper

Task	Purpose	Frequency
Proposal	Groups bidding for topic with a written proposal	Approximately one week to complete
Outline	Bringing together students' ideas, including newly acquired information, and organizing ideas into a coherent flow	Throughout the writing process, but at least one week for developing original outline
First draft	Producing rough draft of paper with every group member's contribution	Approximately 3 weeks to complete
Reciprocal teaching paper	Students using RT to edit and revise	Approximately 4–5 hour sessions
Jigsaw	Students teaching paper through jigsaw process	Approximately 2 hours per group
Revise	Incorporating jigsaw suggestions and revisions	One week after jigsaw

tion, in addition to collecting writing samples, I audiotaped all participant structures daily for 6 weeks to see the connection between what students discussed and what they wrote. On alternate days, I conducted observations of each of the four focal students.

Making Time

To make time in my teaching for observations I did many things. Ingenuity is a key component for any teacher researcher. Sometimes I "swapped" time with a colleague: She took charge of my students, freeing me to observe my four research participants, and later I would provide her the same assistance. At other times,

I assigned independent small-group work to my entire class, giving me the opportunity to observe. These observation periods were usually 45 minutes in length. As an observer, I limited my interactions with all students; if any student asked to talk to me during these periods, I reminded them of my role and arranged to meet them during lunch.

Data collection is one of the trickiest areas for teachers engaging in research. Finding ways to balance the demands of teaching and looking deeply at one's own practice is hard. Teacher researchers address this in many ways. For example, when collecting observation notes some teachers carry a pad, an Alpha-Smart, or a laptop computer. Vivian Paley (1986) set a tape recorder on the table where students were composing. Sometimes I would charge the students with taking notes themselves and then look at what they thought was important. Finding times to look included making deals with other teachers, having students work in small groups, and, best, engaging the students' help.

Getting Permission and Protecting Student Identity

Student work is essential data in all teacher inquiries. It is critical for teachers doing research in their classroom, and in particular when collecting student work, to get signed permission forms from both parents and students. Because teacher research is a regular part of my practice, at the beginning of each school year I send home a form to parents explaining that I plan to document learning in my classroom by doing teacher research. I tell them I am interested in understanding how students learn to read, write, and speak. I ask parents to consider allowing their child to participate in my research, always making it abundantly clear that they have every right to say no.

Parents also have access to any and all publications that discuss and/or show their child. In fact, my practice is to make any publications resulting from my research or the research generated by me and by my students a part of the ever-growing classroom library. This practice is extremely important to my students. On more than one occasion returning students checked to make sure that their research was not only in the classroom library but also cited in other people's work.

Any data such as audio- or videotape that had voices or images of my students is carefully stored in my home so that there is no risk of this raw data being seen by untrained eyes. Maintaining student anonymity is a serious responsibility of any teacher engaging in research.

Making Sense of the Data

Collecting the data was only part of the process. Once the data had been collected, I needed to have a systematic way to look at my findings in order to theorize about what I was seeing. This study represented a close look at the interplay between text and context, between the texts my students were reading and writing and the process by which they were doing it. My research documented the changes of four individual students; it also documented how they worked collaboratively in a small group to advance their literacy skills.

To make sense out of my data, I developed a system for sorting, drawing conclusions, and developing theories. Once this system was in place, I looked across data to identify themes and patterns. First, I looked across all the data for general trends and patterns. Then I repeated the process for each of the four students individually. I followed these steps in analyzing my data:

- Distilled my notes and pulled out common and uncommon occurrences
- Examined all writing samples
- Matched the writing samples up with the data on composing during participant structures
- Examined talk of students while composing, how each revised, and how and when each presented work publicly
- Taped and transcribed all reciprocal teaching lessons because I was also interested in how each learned to read
- Considered how each participated in small-group and whole-class meetings, helped others or received help, and what that meant
- Looked at if or how each used the reading strategies and which strategy was more helpful
- Examined data for evidence of change over time in ability to read, write, and speak in English
- Looked at how what they were thinking impacted communication and/or comprehension.

Once I completed looking at each student individually, I looked across all four students to see what they had in common and what was different. Some of questions I asked as I analyzed the data included the following:

- How might one student's authoritative stance on a particular subject influence another's text?
- How might a student's willingness to collaborate provide another student the comfort level needed to compose a particularly difficult piece?
- How did using words from other people's published text serve as a tool that some students used to elaborate their own ideas?

Through the unpacking of my data, I charted the journey of the four focal students as they learned to communicate in text and talk.

The best way to explain this process is through example. I invite you into my classroom and into my research. In reading the following narrative, consider how all the parts that I have described thus far come together to allow for this window into the world of my classroom.

Learning from My Students

Every classroom is a tapestry of events, people, and experience; therefore, the challenge for any teacher researcher is to use the best analytic tools to observe the complex detail of such a finely woven cloth, making those observations available for reflection, response, and action. In the process, more questions always arise, such as the following:

- How do changes I make in my classroom affect learning?
- How do students change as readers, writers, and thinkers?
- What is the nature of those changes?
- Are they the right changes?
- How do I know?

These questions demand descriptive answers, ones that paint a picture of particular students in a unique classroom. In this section I describe my attempt to make sense of my own practice. It is what happened when I carefully put together all the pieces of the puzzle I have thus far described. This is one example. Ceci in Chapter 3 and Diane in Chapter 4 used the same framework to govern their ways of conducting research, but with very different results. As you read, imagine and even invent what your own research might look like.

Radical Restructuring—Fostering a Community of Learners

After teaching for several years, always at the same grade level and with a similar population of students, I was feeling something I am sure anyone reading this book has felt at one time or another in their teaching career. I was frustrated with the way teaching—and therefore learning—happened in my classroom. I did not feel I was creating, orchestrating, or providing the kind of environment that would allow my students to do the quality of work I knew they were capable of producing. Quite literally at that moment Ann Brown and Joe Campione entered my life. They were working on a curriculum called Fostering a Community of Learners (Brown, 1994; Brown & Campione, 1994). Together with Doris Ash, an expert biology teacher, they were creating a dilemma-based curriculum. They needed two things from me: an urban classroom and an expert in teaching reading, writing, thinking, and speaking. I could supply both things. Thus began one of the most profound collaborations of my professional career. Together with my students, who were cocreators, we developed a curriculum that none of us could have imagined or invented on our own. And I found the context for my research (see Brown et al., 1993).

The Fostering a Community of Learners (FCL) curriculum, immensely challenging and engaging, is framed by a set of principles designed to create classrooms where interacting activities result in building a self-consciously aware and reflective learning environment. In other words, all participants understand that the curriculum, ways to participate, and required products are all intentionally designed so that all become stronger, more capable learners. To accomplish this goal, we conceived of learning as a social process that "occurs as people participate in shared endeavors with others" (Rogoff, 1994, p. 2) and operated from the Vygotskian (1978) perspective that appropriation is what accounts for development and development is facilitated by communication in talk and text.

A set of ritualized practices facilitated students' learning in the company of each other. Students were motivated to learn to read by a desire to acquire deep knowledge because the content was specifically chosen for its high appeal and engaging qualities. Writing and talk were vehicles for distributing expertise, expressing opinions, communicating, and teaching. Reading connected all with the wisdom of outside others.

At its simplest level, FCL was composed of three key parts:

1. Students engaged in independent and group *research* on some aspect of an overarching topic of inquiry. For example, the whole class might be studying why animals become endangered, and each individual group would study a particular animal. Taken together, the students' work builds a body of knowledge about endangered animals.
2. Mastery of the whole topic was ultimately the responsibility of all members of the class. This required students to *share* their expertise with classmates.
3. Sharing created the motivation to *do* something with what was learned.

The three activities—*research* in order to *share* in order to *do* a consequential task—were all done in the service of each other. Students in collaboration with teachers and other students constructed new understanding together. Acumen in the new domains grew and changed as our collective knowledge became more sophisticated.

In this interactive environment, each student performed as a serious scholar. Daily classroom activities resembled a graduate seminar. Aware that not all people learn or respond in the same way, we (teachers and students) intentionally fostered an accepting environment that invited risk taking (Britton, 1987). Instruction was based on the principle that, as teacher, I needed to respond at opportune moments to the needs of the students. The students, in collaboration with their peers, and through engagement with demanding materials, constructed new understanding.

The Context

As a mechanism for inviting you into my world, I want to explain a bit about the school where I taught and my students; I have already explained how I organized my classroom for learning. Each of these items are important contexts that informed my research and learning. A big part of making any research accessible is to carefully set the context for the reader.

The School. Located in the San Francisco Bay Area, my school was part of a district that had very wide socioeconomic, race, and linguistic diversity. The majority of our student population was on free and reduced-price lunch, and most conducted their lives at school in two or more languages. Our school was small, and because the teaching staff enjoyed a good reputation, many parents chose to place their children there. Without question, the main reason our school was so wonderful was that it was populated by students who loved to dream, create, and explore.

My Students. My students' abilities and experience with writing and reading were as diverse as their languages, making it imperative that I, as their teacher, seriously consider issues facing bilingual and bidilectical students as they are in the process of acquiring multifaceted academic literacy skills in English. To understand more about these complex issues, I narrowed the lens of my research to focus on four bilingual girls, each from a different language background. English was a second (sometimes third) language for all the girls. Two of them were recent immigrants and spoke virtually no English upon arriving at my school. The other two had spent all of their school years in American schools; yet these two did not display the writing and speaking competencies required for full participation in class discussions and academic writing. My choice of these four students was by no means random. I chose them because they were typical of the kind of bilingual student in my classroom but also because a careful study of these four students would serve as valuable, usable knowledge to inform my work with other bilingual students.

As explained earlier, the science curriculum these students worked on was in the domain of biology, specifically endangered species. The learning activities provided a variety of dialectical contexts, and a tension existed between the text (what the students read and wrote) and the context (the interactive process). In other words, as students encountered more complex biology, they needed to acquire more complex literacy skills and English to deal with the subject. Text and context, linked in authentic purpose, worked in tandem, constraining or enhancing each other at different times (Vygotsky, 1978). For that reason, I intentionally watched my students during all literacy events such as composing, small-group and whole-class discussions, and reciprocal teaching sessions.

Reciprocal Teaching (RT) is a reading comprehension strategy designed by Annemarie Palinscar and Ann Brown (1984). During an RT session, students work together in small groups of four to six. Using a discussion format, they read paragraph by paragraph while employing four metacognitive strategies. The strategies are summarizing, predicting, clarifying, and questioning. Once students learn the protocol, they take turns acting as teachers during 12 to 15 sequential sessions. The principle behind this strategy is that a close reading combined with the execution of a set of metacognitive reading strategies often used automatically by successful readers will allow students to learn how to read for understanding. In this study I used RT for building comprehension competence as well as revision skills. Therefore, it was essential that I observed my focal students during implementation of RT so that I could find out if my hypothesis as to its usefulness was correct.

Case Studies

What follows is a summary of the case studies of the four students. Embedded in the case studies are some examples of times I watched the students to find answers to my research questions. Following these summaries, I present results of my research and how the findings changed my practice based on new understandings of how bilingual students learn.

Bobbie. Having immigrated to this country when she was 4 years old, Bobbie was trilingual in Cambodian, Laotian, and English. All of her schooling was in the United States, and Bobbie preferred English over her other languages, although she periodically expressed concern about forgetting the other languages. At home she spoke to her parents and elders in Laotian and Cambodian; however, she conversed primarily in English with her school-age siblings. With high scores on the district language assessments, Bobbie no longer qualified for language support services, such as pullout programs in English as a Second Language (ESL).

Though successful in most school subjects, Bobbie lacked the necessary writing skills to be successful in high school. I did not understand why her writing skills were so much less developed when compared to her other academic skills. Was it a question of understanding the material? A language difficulty? A lack of practice and opportunity to write? To answer my questions, I observed Bobbie during a variety of literacy activities beginning with reciprocal teaching. During the first four RT sessions, I observed Bobbie's participation increase dramatically. She spontaneously volunteered responses to questions that were posed to the whole group. The following example records Bobbie attempting to help another English language learner clarify the meaning of a word in a text they had read about peregrine falcon chicks:

Mikiyung: What's fewer?
Bobbie: Littler, smaller. . . .
Teacher: Not as many.
Mihee: (*reading the sentence*) "There have been fewer and
     fewer hungry chicks." What this mean?
Bobbie: They have been smaller and smaller.
Teacher: Smaller numbers means not as many.

This exchange helped me understand something of Bobbie's struggle. When she attempted to define the word *fewer* for Mikiyung she misinterpreted the nuanced difference between *fewer* and *smaller*. Often when a bilingual student reaches a basic level of sophistication in his or her verbal abilities in a second language, it is assumed that the language learner understands what is being said (Cummins, 1981). But basic oral proficiency may obscure gaps in linguistic knowledge. Reciprocal teaching sessions provided me a way of uncovering these. Without my intervention in the RT session recorded above, the students might have concluded (erroneously) that peregrine falcons were having smaller chicks instead of there being fewer chicks. The presence of the more experienced speaker (in this case me) meant that the subtleties of the text would not be overlooked and that the children, even those at a high level of competence in English, had the opportunity to learn the meaning and function of a new, more sophisticated concept.

Reciprocal teaching also provided a structure for revising writing. As a group, the students "RTed" their completed writing, using the RT strategies to respond to each other's texts, ask questions, and clarify meaning. While engaged in "RTing" a fellow student's paper, the students tried to summarize the author's thesis and predict the intention of the work. While examining Bobbie's writing, her peers grappled with the complicated process of how pollution enters into a whale's physiology through the food chain. In her first draft, Bobbie made the following argument:

> Pollution is also causing whales to die. Since the ocean
> is dirty it cause some of their food to die or their habit in
> the ocean being distroyed. It is also because the whales
> food chain is broken so the whales have less food to eat.
> Their are not enough food to go around for the whales.

From the discussion that followed, I observed that Bobbie had a greater understanding of the material than she had exhibited in her writing. The members of her research group and I questioned her about the meaning of her text, seeking clarification on some points. In her revision, Bobby made herself more fully understood, inserting logical transitions and needed information in the gaps that existed in the previous draft. Without the discussion that had gone on at the appropriate time, she could not have made such substantive revisions. The talk surrounding her piece provided useful vocabulary that she appropriated to clarify her meaning. Clear enunciation from a native speaker of English allowed her to hear ending sounds (e.g., the "s" in *causes*) that previously went unnoticed. At the end of the discussion Bobbie made the following adjustments:

> Pollution is also causing whales to die. Since the ocean is
> dirty it causes some of the whale's food to get dirty. For
> example, DDT gets on the algae and the krill eat the al-
> gae. When the whales eat the krill they might get sick be-

cause they will get DDT in their system. Remember that the whales eat a lot of krill.

By the end of the semester, Bobbie fully participated in her RT group. She also willingly offered comments in the more public forum of the whole-class discussions, conversing with people with whom she had little association. During the first half of the year she had not participated in the scientific discussions with these students, yet after several RT sessions she began to speak spontaneously without any prompting.

Jessie. Also trilingual, Jessie spoke Cantonese, Mandarin, and English. Cantonese was the primary home language. Neither of her parents spoke English. Jessie's parents strongly encouraged her to maintain her knowledge of Mandarin and Cantonese and provided numerous situations in the home for her to read, write, and speak these languages. Jessie's father, though currently working as a skilled laborer, had been a university-trained zoologist. He considered academic literacy very important.

Jessie had spent her entire school career at the same school. Like Bobbie, she had tested out of ESL services the previous year. A capable speaker of English, Jessie could express herself successfully on most occasions. In writing, however, she experienced difficulty communicating. When asked to evaluate her own writing ability, she wrote:

> I think writing is kind of hard for me, because sometimes
> I don't know what to write. Writing a lot is hard for me
> too like I have to write two pages or more. Sharing my
> writing is what I hate most about writing because some-
> times it embares Me and I think they might think my
> story is stupid.

Despite such self-criticism, Jessie considered English her strongest language. She was concerned, however, that when she got confused about a word, she sometimes reverted to a Cantonese word without even knowing it. What she described was not code switching between two languages to enhance communication (Valdés-Fallis, 1978), but the interference of one language with another.

The RT sessions were most beneficial to Jessie's writing and revising skills. Prior to participation in the FCL project, Jessie wrote as little as possible, probably because of her difficulty with it but also because she had not been in classrooms where there was a strong emphasis on writing. After overcoming the initial anxiety of facing the blank page, weekly discussions using the RT format helped Jessie extend and revise her writing. This is her first attempt at writing an introduction to her group's project:

> We are the Dolphin group. Are indangered animal is the Whales, we shared with lots question. We have found out lots abouts Whales, but some of our question are still not answered. We hope you will take time to read this report and consider are suggestion to help save the Whales and keep are environment, and ocean clean.

During conversations about the writing, I asked the group to be more specific about what "lots of questions" meant. In a discussion that followed, the members of the group explained that they had questions about "different kinds of whales." Jessie also explained that while they had learned a number of things, they still had a lot of questions that were not answered. I explained that research, by definition, deals with many unanswered questions. All that she needed to do as the author was make it explicit that this was just the beginning of an ongoing study. Also, talk about the text afforded an opportunity to point out the difference between *are* and *our.* This is an easy mistake for bilingual students to make because in spoken form they sound so similar. Though Jessie hated to share her writing with the whole class, she grew more comfortable with it because her group members were her close friends and because she came to see writing-conference sessions as valuable revision times.

Timely scaffolding of new ideas is an important support mechanism for the language learner (Cazden, 2001; Fillmore, 1979). We dealt with general issues of composing as well as subtle nuances of meaning embedded in the language. After several writing conferences including her group members, Jessie modified her piece of writing in the following manner:

> Our group is studying whales. We want to know why whales are becoming endangered. We began our research with lots of questions. We have found out some of the

answers, but some of the questions are still not answered. So we hope that you will keep in mind that this is just the beginning of our study.

In our research we have looked at different kinds of whales, we did this because we wanted to show which kinds of whales are more endangered and why that is true. All whales are on the endangered list, but some are in more trouble then others.

Regularly scheduled writing conferences went beyond criticizing surface features of the writing and focused on meaning, enabling Jessie to create a text that was excellent for her purpose and audience. This discussion also helped Jessie realize the complexity and depth of her thinking.

Mihee and Mikiyung. Mihee and Mikiyung were sisters who immigrated to the United States from Korea a few months before entering my class. At the beginning of the year, they were very hesitant to speak the little bit of English they knew. Nobody in their family spoke English, and the two sisters relied entirely on school contexts and social situations for their target language input. Despite their hesitancy to speak English, the girls were eager to learn, and they practiced English at home with a self-tutoring cassette tape program. By the end of the school year, they had made sufficient progress to make themselves understood in most situations, socially and academically.

Though Mihee and Mikiyung were eager to learn English, the language frustrated them. These children left a country where they had full command of the language and entered a strange country whose language intimidated them (Lindfors, 1987; Paley, 1986). By their own account, both children experienced much success in Korean schools; they now perceived themselves as able learners who could not communicate. Of her school experience, Mikiyung said, "In Korea many people told me that I was a good writer, but now I am a girl who is a little troubled because I can't speak English. I have been in America for 10 months." Her sister Mihee admitted similar feelings of frustration.

Mihee and Mikiyung's participation in the FCL project offered them many opportunities to learn English. The small-group discussions enabled them to hear English spoken in a conversational manner (Fillmore, 1991; Grosjean, 1982; Mohan, 1986). Moreover, because their partners Bobbie and Jessie were multilingual themselves, they took pains to modify their speech to help Mihee and Mikiyung understand (Fillmore, 1992). Because these girls chose to be in this particular group, they felt comfortable taking risks as they used the only language common to them all (Swain, 1985).

The RT sessions offered distinct benefits for bilingual students who had different learning needs. The small-group format of the RT sessions encouraged Mikiyung and Mihee to participate; they were also encouraged by the nonthreatening, "bite-sized" amount of text presented during each session. After reading each paragraph, discussion followed. The predictable routine of the RT sessions enabled the girls to know what was expected of them, reducing anxiety and increasing their participation (Fillmore, 1991). During these sessions, the sisters had plenty of time to clarify words and concepts they didn't understand and to relate the text to their own life experiences. The format of the RT sessions gave them the necessary opportunities to interrupt discussions to ask for clarification of a word or sentence. In fact, in the very first RT group and with each continuing RT session, Mihee and Mikiyung asked for more and more definitions of words. Initially their questions focused on procedures of the RT session:

> *Mikiyung*: What *prediction* mean?
> *Teacher*: It tells you what is going to happen next.
> *Mikiyung*: What *summarize*?
> *Bobbie*: It tells you a little about what is in the paragraph.
> *Mihee*: What *clarify*?
> *Jessie*: Making it clear.
> *Mihee*: I get it.

It is difficult to know if Mihee or Mikiyung really "got it"—whether they really understood the nuances of the RT process. But what was clear is that they did see that there was a ritualistic way of participating in the conversation, and the ritualized practices allowed them to begin to understand the text.

During one session, Mikiyung asked the meaning of the word *extinct*. Bobbie, the RT leader of the group, explained the idea of an endangered species. After some discussion, Mikiyung understood the difference between *extinct* and *endangered* and related the term to an experience she had in Korea: "Long time ago, they killed tigers, so no more tigers in Korea. So Korean people like tigers, but no more tigers. So we can't see, only zoos."

In the RT sessions like those I quote above, I observed the sisters making greater and more complex use of the English language. They discerned basic conventions of writing and assimilated them into their knowledge of the language. For example, when they recognized that the main idea was generally found in the beginning of a paragraph, they were often able to identify main ideas and summarize a short text. These reading strategies gave the sisters a starting point in writing their paper about whales. They used information acquired in texts as the starting point for an idea they themselves wanted to elaborate on paper. This is a sample of Mihee's work at this stage:

> Whales live in the ocean like fish, and they swim around and hunt fish in the ocean like fish. It is warm-blooded with a body temperature that is more or less the same all the time. The babies of mammals are born alive instead of hatched from eggs. And the babies take milk from thire mother. Scientists call whales ceteans which means whales.

This example of Mihee's writing was not consistent with her spoken language. The terms she used in this passage were much more sophisticated in syntax and lexical items than what normally appeared in her talk. What was important at this stage was not the "direct" authorship of the words, but that the child was able to convey the meaning that she intended. Up to this point both children had written everything in Korean. In this instance they went directly to the book and looked for the information that they needed and then placed it in their paper. This first step served as a bridge to other compositions, ones that would ultimately be composed of Mihee's own words. But this way of using other people's text is an extension of Fillmore's (1979) use of formulaic speech. Mihee used other people's words to gain entrance into this discourse community. Later, as she became a more proficient speaker of science discourse, she needed less assistance.

Several weeks and many drafts later, the girls' writing became less dependent on using others' words. They began to formulate their own ideas, building on information they gleaned in their reading and in group discussions. Here is an example of Mihee's text at this stage:

Eating

Whales eats lots of food. One of the many thins they
eat are krills. They eat about two tons a day. The baby
whales drink the mothers milk about forty time a day.
That's why they so big. Whales eat krill because there
are so many krill in the world. They also eat krill because
krills are mostly found in cold places. One way whales
are indangered is because there is not enough feed to go
around for the whales. This is the problem we have to
solve it will be hard but we need to save the whales.
THE END

Mihee has made a major shift. This was her first attempt to compose original text. Taking ideas she read and talked about previously, she speculated on her own about the fate of the whales.
She also incorporated some of the community's writing traditions
by placing the title at the beginning of her piece and tacking the
words "THE END" at the end. Most important, she had the confidence and wherewithal to put her own ideas down on paper for
all to read.

How Research Informed My Practice

Teacher research was a rich experience, one that informed my
practice in multiple ways. Primarily, it gave me an opportunity
to question the context and the conditions of my teaching. In the
process of shaping my own inquiry, I learned from others who had
investigated similar issues. To deepen my understanding of what
was important and necessary when teaching bilingual students, I
kept company (through talk and text) with folks who studied the
nuances and intricacies of second language learning. In reorga-
nizing my classroom, I joined a group of like-minded people to
understand and implement optimal conditions to support learning in a community of learners environment. Careful preparation
before embarking on my study helped me set the stage. Having
a plan for collecting and analyzing my data allowed me to learn
about building an environment to support learning and to under-

stand what kinds of curriculum and participa
language and content acquisition. In the end, m
my future teaching in profound ways.

Specifically, I came to understand the value of
one is in the process of acquiring another language. In
ing my classroom, I built in ways for my students to co
in the choice of their own research while investigating co
and engaging topics. This created an integrity that gave the
dents real ownership. Reading, writing, and talk became a way
bridge new understandings while answering each student's own
compelling questions. Communication with peers—so vital to
this process—created new opportunities for language learning.

The cohesive, integrated curriculum brought the elements of
the classroom together in a meaningful way. Ideas gleaned from
whole-class discussions later appeared in written text with intro-
ductory phrases such as "We have learned from class discussion."
Reciprocal teaching, the structure, group size, strategies, and formulaic speech provided a way for emergent literates to access
complicated text, while learning the discourse of the community.
Multiple group configurations and the ritualistic function of the
activities aided in language learning. The predictable participant
structures, like RT, enabled students to anticipate what was expected, thereby giving the students more choice of how and when
they would enter into the discourse community. Moreover, antici-
pation of events allowed the children to prepare for those things
that were forthcoming. Preparation diminished anxiety.

The intimacy of the small group offered opportunities to talk
freely and expand ideas at length. Equally important was the nur-
turing of untested theories. The safety of being among the company
of peers with whom they chose to study provided the girls with a
place where they could try out their wildest flights of fancy.

A predictable and transparent way of organizing the writing
process was helpful to all emergent literates in any discourse (Fillmore, 1979) and made a seemingly overwhelming task (writing
a whole research paper) doable. Once students understood the
papers they wrote as a place to display new knowledge, the writing had a compelling purpose. Then the process of getting their
ideas down on paper and pulling together the multitudes of experiences and thoughts for the purpose of sharing their ideas was
extremely powerful (Dyson, 1993).

the language learners in my
ultiple entry points into the
single element of this proj-
really stellar paper. It was
s they came together. One
t on the other (Brown &
as were never just formu-
nstructed as the children
d thinking together (Dy-

ystem of checks and balances
classroom teacher, with ample opportu-
many windows into the child's learning experience.
was this ability to observe the social and academic events, as
they took place in the classroom, under a variety of circumstances
that gave me a way to more fully assess the language needs and
to ultimately meet those needs. As students proceeded through
the program, they came to know more about the learning process
in general and were better able to understand their own newly
acquired knowledge (Brown & Campione, 1994).

My role as teacher researcher created a way for me to have
many windows into the lives of my students. Through systematic
inquiry, driven by my need to understand the complexities of my
own classroom, I came to have a richer, deeper understanding of
my students' worlds. And like the experience of the students with
their own research, systematic inquiry allowed me to have new
ways of seeing and knowing. I could see Mikiyung and Mihee
become more adventurous as writers. I could correct subtle mis-
conceptions that Bobbie and Jessie had about certain words. But
most important, I could experience firsthand these young women
developing into capable scholars.

41

CHAPTER 3

USING NARRATIVE

AS TEACHER RESEARCH

Learning About Language and Life Through Personal Stories

CECI LEWIS

DIXIE GOSWAMI: *In her foreword to* The Best for Our Children: Critical Perspectives on Literacy for Latino Students *(Reyes & Halcon, 2001), Sonia Nieto says the book "is unique not only because of what it says about Latino students but also because of who is saying it" (p. ix), in this case, Latino educators. Ceci Lewis's research is also unique because of who she is: a Latina woman, a self-described "border brat," a teacher in a border community for a number of years, and a woman with connections. At about the time that Ceci, teaching Latino students, came to understand that the distance between herself and her students was not a natural asset to her or to them, she had the occasion to attend a small conference sponsored for practitioner researchers by the Spencer Foundation. There she talked to Lusanda Mayikana from South Africa, Michael Armstrong, and Courtney Cazden, among others, about what kept second language learners from talking in class and writing in school. Over a period of about 6 months Ceci continued talking, mostly online, about these issues, and an inquiry group formed, fluid at first but becoming solid and stable early on. Expectations about what they would learn from language acquisition stories told in the form of online dialogue journals, open to response and interpretation by every member of the group, constituted their assumptions. Michael Armstrong's fully developed practice of read-*

ing children's stories interpretively constituted the methodology that began with establishing relationships of respect across age, race, and other boundaries, and moved to writing and sharing the language acquisition stories and meeting to construct knowledge, insights, and questions about what they knew. Every member of the inquiry group, including students, did every task: They wrote and interpreted stories; they set agendas; they questioned conclusions; and they strategized ways to disseminate, sustain, and extend their work.

Here is a model for teachers who believe that young people and adults must work together to create knowledge and insights about critical literacy in the twenty-first century. Their inquiry was about narration and language acquisition, but it touched upon bilingual education, and the rich experiences and linguistic resources that children and adults bring to school. Moreover, Ceci's study provides a close-up look at children, young people, and adults functioning as full, active, creative, ethical participants in a digital environment. Khulekani, a 20-year-old Xhosa student who was part of the inquiry team wrote this as the formal part of the study ended: "Just listen to what we have to say!"

Honoring the knowledge and skills of Khulekani and other young coresearchers in public and professional settings places Ceci's work in an intellectual tradition represented by advocates whose backgrounds and experiences are as diverse as those of the students who are part of Ceci's inquiry group. Shirley Brice Heath (1999), Steve Goodman (2003), and Barbara Cervone (2006) are among those who claim that today's youth are media makers and cultural producers who are acquiring skills and knowledge (in and out of school) for full cultural participation. As one of their assumptions, they expect young people to help create an urgently needed pool of knowledge about literacy, digital media, and civic engagement.

In the twenty-first century it's entirely possible to imagine a version of Ceci's chapter, complete with links, images, and audio, perhaps as an interactive Web site, free and accessible to all who wish to add their own language-learning stories. Ceci's story and the inquiry she recounts, grounded in constructivist theories and practices and committed to Emig's (1983) inquiry paradigm as a dynamic formulation, helps us reconceptualize literacy research in the digital age, when the notion of "literacy as freedom" has implications for survival.

Born and raised on the Arizona-Mexico border, language has always taken a center stage in my life. For me, and for my language story, the words of Gloria Anzaldúa (1987) provide a context: "The U.S.-Mexican border *es una herida abierta* where the Third World grates against the first and bleeds. And before a scab forms it hemorrhages again, the lifeblood of two worlds merging to form a third country—a border culture" (p. 3). She refers to the borderlands as an area where two worlds grate against each other. These lands often overlapped each other; sometimes they competed against each other; and more often than not, they contradicted each other. Although language and life intertwine, on the border they often clash. Nowhere is the collision more evident than in the English classroom in an Arizona public school.

While enrolled in teacher training courses, I naively believed that being Latina, speaking two languages, and teaching in my own backyard would give me an edge with my students. I knew the country, the climate, the language; and I was "one of them." By bringing this personal experience to the English classroom, I felt that I could help alleviate the "scarring" that takes place for my students whose primary language is Spanish and their secondary language, English. Supplied with the best of intentions and a personal awareness and understanding of the frustration of learning a second language, I eagerly entered the classroom with high hopes and dreams.

Unfortunately, my good intentions and personal experience did not prepare me for the reality of what I encountered. Addressing Spanish-speaking students in their primary language did not serve to make them more comfortable in the classroom. Instead, it served to isolate them from other classmates. The political, personal, and pedagogical realities of language proved to be far more complex than I had naively believed, especially in the politically charged Southwest.

FACTORS GOVERNING MY GAZE

My experience teaching English along the border between southern Arizona and northern Mexico has been exceptionally fascinating and intriguing. It has been my observation that the physical proximity to the border itself becomes a distinguishing factor in the acceptance level of a second language in the classroom. When I began teaching in Bisbee, Arizona, which is situated less than five miles from the international border, the use of Spanish was a common, everyday, every-class situation. However, when I moved to Tombstone, which is situated approximately 30 miles north of the same border, I found that many students view the use of Spanish as "un-American" or wrong. This short distance represents the movement from Anzaldúa's "third country—a border culture" to the more dominant culture of the United States. Sadly, I cannot count the times students at Tombstone High School have told me, "Speak English, this is America." My experience with this, whether it is in the hallways during breaks or in my classroom as I help a student has resulted in a heart-wrenching understanding of the political implications of language and the fear associated with using a language other than English in the public school setting. Yet my personal experience, pedagogical training, and gut feeling all said that if I spoke to them in Spanish, they would be more inclined to respond and feel at home in the English classroom. Added to that personal distress is the political strain from Arizona's "English Only" law, which passed on November 7, 2000. It states that students, whose primary language is other than English, will have 2 years in a sheltered English classroom before they must transition into English-only courses, regardless of their English competency levels. Therefore, it was with great trepidation that I found myself trying to ease the academic frustration of students whose primary language was Spanish.

FINDING AND JOINING A TRADITION

My students were not the only ones who experienced isolation. As a teacher in a rural school, my intuition and training told me one thing about language acquisition, my state education board mandated another, and my colleagues, struggling to stay afloat, were focused on other educational issues. As a result, I found myself looking outside of my immediate communities for solutions to the language problems that plagued my classroom. Fortunately, my frustrations and fears were alleviated when I attended a Spencer Foundation Teacher Research Conference at the Bread Loaf School of English in Vermont during June 2000. It was in this academically rich environment that I learned how I could use my experience to examine, through teacher research, what it means to be a speaker of more than one language.

The participants of the conference, educators from all over the United States and other countries, including South Africa, gathered in small groups to discuss issues that teachers could research in their classrooms. Since the groups were formed by the interests of the participants, I found myself surrounded with others who shared the same passion for language and learning that I did. The seeds of this project were planted as I sat in my discussion group and learned from the other participants in the group their experiences in the classroom and with their students.

Much like Marty's work demonstrates (see Chapter 2), my research was inspired by my own need to understand and clarify the phenomena in my classroom. Through my experience at the conference, what had once been a nebulous, nagging feeling began to take shape into a structured, student-centered examination of language issues. Writing the proposal for the Spencer Foundation Research Grant truly helped to solidify the research process and deepened my capacity to understand the language challenges facing my students.

It was at this conference that I found myself connecting with like-minded individuals who shared my passion and concern for language, even though we came from very different communities with very different curricular demands. Michael Armstrong, English primary school headmaster and expert on narrative, brought to the table his expertise on the narratives that students write. Lusanda Mayikana, South African college professor and multiple language speaker, brought her personal expertise on language acquisition and life in a country that recognizes 11 official languages. I brought to the project a desire to learn how to help students bridge the gap between what they know and what they need to know. I discovered that finding compatible individuals with whom to work on research is important. When you are thinking about a teacher research project and looking for possible research partners, consider colleagues in your school, faculty at your local university, and members of professional organizations.

For me, having distance from my classroom and being surrounded by colleagues provided a space where I could begin to explore the dissonance I experienced in my classroom. It was in this network that I learned how to bounce off of others ideas that had formed in my mind. It was in this neutral area that I learned the value of vocalizing my observations, hunches, and ideas so that a research plan could begin to form. It was in this neutral area that I learned the value of probing an issue that not only deeply impacted the lives of my students and myself, but warranted exploration.

With the help of my research colleagues, we explored what it meant to acquire another language. By describing and explaining my classroom and community to my colleagues, I was better able to see for myself exactly what I was experiencing. This type of reflective experience became a valuable starting point for our project.

For a classroom teacher to become engaged in a research project always seems to be a bit daunting. When and how will I ever find the time to research, document, and write? What I learned, however, is that classroom teachers are in the best position to do the research. We are right in the middle of the education process! Becoming a teacher researcher not only makes sense, it is a necessity. In the remainder of this chapter, I will walk you through the research process as it pertains to our project. I will explain how we got started, what happened, and what we learned.

Developing a Set of Assumptions

Our research group was motivated by the language experiences and theories of academic Victor Villanueva, who in his text *Bootstraps: From an American Academic of Color* (1993), wrote: "Biculturalism does not mean to me an equal ease with two cultures. Rather, biculturalism means the tensions within, which are caused by being unable to deny the old or the new" (p. 39). We wanted to identify the tensions our students were experiencing, which either helped or hindered their ability to succeed academically in a predominantly English-speaking forum.

Coupled with the personal tension of straddling two cultures, we also recognized the political tension of educating students in the public school setting. I truly began to understand how frightening the language issues in my state were becoming. In less than 5 months my home state would actually pass a proposition that restricted and limited language usage, and I was feeling the political heat as an instructor who knows that the more languages a student speaks, the more opportunities are available to him or her. Primarily because Michael Armstrong and Lusanda Mayikana did not teach in the United States, they were able to offer a detached perspective of education and language policies in our country, while also looking critically at the language policies in their own countries. Working with these diverse global insights, we recognized the importance of the knowledge students bring with them. According to Guadalupe Valdés (2001), "Teachers must work to help students develop their own voices—not what has been termed the 'babble' of communicative language teaching, but rather voices that are tied to a vision of possibilities" (p. 158). As a research group, we recognized the importance of having the students teach us what it means to acquire another language.

Finally, drawing on the work of Cynthia Ballenger (1999) and Vivian Paley (1981), we determined that having students write their language stories would be the most effective way for us to begin gathering our data. Both of these researchers center their work on what the students can tell us about what they know. This inside-out approach goes directly to source for information—the students. By looking closely at student work and listening closely to what students say, teachers can become better informed educators.

FORMING OUR QUESTIONS

Identifying our research questions became the next step in the research process. Based on our assumptions and informed by the theories surrounding language acquisition, we formulated the questions that would guide our research.

Together we created a set of research questions that we felt would help us focus on the issues that surrounded bilingualism and deeply affected our students. Having taken Michael Armstrong's class at Bread Loaf School of English, The Origin of Narratives and the Narratives of Origin, I was convinced that storytelling could serve as a key to unlock our students' stories and thus enable self-discovery. Through the analysis of personal narratives, as researchers, we could analyze the text our students produced to learn what language acquisition truly entailed (Armstrong, 1999). Initially, my goal was to try to understand why these students remained silenced in the classroom. We all felt that by sharing our language stories online in an electronic conference, we could make some sense out of what it means to be bilingual— to live in two worlds. We recognized that we had two main focuses: bilingualism and the use of narrative.

The guiding questions we developed and agreed to discuss via an electronic network include:

- How can narrative in the classroom and online help to give voice to limited-English speakers who have been silenced?
- How does the language of the classroom affect the language and the culture of the community?
- How does the culture of the classroom empower students to be change agents beyond the classroom and beyond the community?

Methodology: Our Ways of Seeing

In order to get our project off the ground, we had to iron out the logistics of this research project. While at the conference, we established the guiding research questions, agreed to the number of research participants, and developed a place and a way to conference. Since we were located on three different continents, the logical means of communication for us was BreadNet, a computer network that allows those affiliated with the Bread Loaf School of English to communicate with each other. There are numerous English teaching blogs available for those looking to find an online community in which to participate. We opened up an electronic conference folder in BreadNet specifically for our work, and that is where the bulk of our communication took place. Inside this conference folder, we established four other folders:

- Student Stories, where all the student work was located
- Teacher Tales, where the teacher researchers posted their stories and "aha moments"
- Student Data, where we posted transcripts of interviews
- Interpretations, where we posted our academic interpretations of specific student work

This organization allowed us the opportunity to keep track of the work we were doing, and eased accessibility when we needed to retrieve any of our work.

Beginning the Project

Once back at our respective sites, Lusanda, Michael, and I agreed that we needed a third classroom to give us a truly cross-generational study. Having admired Mary Guerrero's work with bilingual elementary students in Lawrence, Massachusetts, we invited her to join our research project. Located on three continents (North America, Africa, and Europe), the final research team included a wide range of ages including fourth graders from Lawrence, Massachusetts; high school students from Tombstone, Arizona; college students from the University of Witwatersrand in Johannesburg, South Africa; and the teacher researchers, Mary, Michael, Lusanda, and I.

My attendance at the Teacher Research Conference, combined with courses I had taken on narrative and my personal experience, all coalesced to enable me to participate in a teacher research project that is a cross-cultural, cross-generational study focused on narrative, language, and identity, set in a revolutionary forum that provided immediate response despite the geographical distances involved.

Let me clarify what I mean by a "revolutionary forum." Utilizing an electronic conference, our research group created a research space where all participants (including students) posted their stories and responses to each other. As a result, not only did we break conventional research protocol by posting our data in a virtual space where the conversation was easily accessible by members of the project, but also the lines between teacher researchers and student subjects quickly blurred as our stories opened up conversations that changed the traditional teacher-student relationship. The cyberspace conversation allowed for members to assume different roles. Fourth graders were not only sharing their experiences with high school and college students, but they were also offering advice and recommendations about language acquisition to the teachers in the project. This ability to recognize and validate each other's responses blew open our expectations of the project as we all became learners together.

By using an electronic conference as the primary storehouse for communication, our work became easily accessible to all members of the researcher team. Cyberspace networks allow for virtual spaces that provide access for more participants. As you think about your own research, consider the logistics:

- Where will you file your notes and observations?
- How accessible will they be?
- Who might be able to access your work?

Putting the Project into Action

Upon returning to our home sites, we identified and invited our student coresearchers. Lusanda opened up the conference to any students who were not only interested in participating but willing to devote the time necessary to do so. My process of recruitment was a bit more direct. I identified second language learners who had puzzled me the previous year. I had taught all three students as sophomores and had found their willingness to participate in classroom discussions either limited or completely absent. Since I was working in a rather small rural school, I knew that I would be having these students in my class again as juniors and seniors; therefore, it was not only convenient, but essential that I follow their progress as they continued their education. Although the research project continues, for the purpose of this chapter, I will focus specifically on the work of one student, Samuel Pacheco, from Tombstone High School, and show how our work together taught me what it means to be bilingual and to teach bilingual students, and how teacher research provided a revolutionary forum for informing my personal practice and enhancing the learning of my students.

SAMUEL'S STORY

Samuel truly puzzled me. He would enter my classroom and immediately grab the daily newspaper. Rarely did he come to class prepared with the required textbook and notebook for the class. Instead, he would open up the newspaper to the want-ad section and begin browsing under the automotive headings, and he would remain there, hidden behind the paper, for as much of the class period as I allowed. Interestingly, although he never seemed to read along with the class, or even do the work while in class, he always turned in all assignments on time and properly done. Most often he would drop off the assignment first thing in the morning although his class did not meet until the end of the day. He scored high on all the unit exams. His writing, although rough, did show promise. Believing that Samuel would be more comfortable speaking to me in Spanish, I began to address him in Spanish; but while he was in the classroom, he never addressed me in Spanish. His replies were always in English—short and even perfunctory at times—but always in English.

First Posting of Stories

After Samuel agreed to work on the project with us, we all began by posting our own language memoirs. I submitted mine first and then gave a copy to each of the students involved in the project. Together during lunch time, the students and I read my entry; we discussed it and found similarities and major differences in our language experiences. From then on, each person posted his or her own reflections and ideas on language. Soon the conference took on its own life and for the next 2 years, we discussed, shared, questioned, wrote, read, and wrote some more. We equally shared in the discussions, and we equally reaped the benefits.

Below is my first entry in the electronic exchange folder. Our language stories served as the seed from which the rest of the exchange grew. By sharing our own personal stories on language acquisition, we (the teacher researchers) not only hoped to get our students to identify and recognize the value of sharing narratives, but also wanted to demonstrate the importance and value of each person's story.

Language Memoir

Finding the proper words and order to tell the story of my own personal language acquisition has proven to be more difficult than I thought. It seems impossible for me to tell my story without going back to my mother and father's language stories. From there, I find myself going to their par-

ents and then I realize that my language story is really very
much their language story. Here goes!

I am first-generation United States American on my father's side and second-generation on my mother's side. My
most recent ancestors all entered the United States from
Mexico. The very name of the country means "mixed"
and so my family history is exactly that—mixed! The first
language both my parents spoke, however, was Spanish.
My mother, Lillian Esther Burgner Durazo, was born to a
father of German American heritage and a mother of Mexican American heritage. Despite the fact that her father was
technically a *gringo* (slang for "white man"), mother's first
language was Spanish and when my grandfather left, the
primary language of the home became Spanish.

My father, Francisco Jose Durazo, always insisted on being called an American of Mexican descent. His family immigrated to the United States when he was 4 years old. His
mother, who lived in the United States for the last 44 years of
her life, never spoke English. I recall only two English terms
she would use: the first was her favorite television character,
"ehStony Burke" and the second was the proclamation of
her citizenship whenever we crossed the border. Although
my grandmother never found it necessary to speak the language of her adopted country, she remained adamant that
her children should.

My childhood memories are filled with admonishments,
which were used to help me correct any mispronunciation:
"The word is *sandwich*—not *sangwich*! *Church*, not *shurch*;
champagne, not *shampagne*." Along with pronunciation lessons were also lessons in proper tone. Being a raucous child,
my mother was forever asking me to "modulate your voice."
All of this energy, which was placed on learning how to
speak proper English, never crossed over into Spanish acquisition. As a matter of fact, Spanish was not spoken in my
home unless one of us kids got into real trouble. Then the
Spanish terms flew out of my mother's mouth with no stop-
ping. It seemed that she only reverted back to her mother
tongue when she was too frustrated to speak "properly."

As I mentioned earlier, my paternal grandmother did
not speak English at all. I don't remember experiencing

any communication problems. There is one story, however, which still haunts me. When I was about 10 or 11 years old, I remember going to my Nani's (Spanish nickname for grandmother) with the sole intent of impressing her with my Spanish. I had never had a class in Spanish and so all I knew about the language was what I had been able to decipher when the adults spoke. (They always spoke in Spanish when they were discussing things they didn't want the children to know about.) So, here I am, all ready to really impress my grandmother. When I spoke, I said, *"Buenas dias, Nani. Como se sientas?"* Well, the next thing I knew, my grandmother was laughing so hard she had tears coming out of her eyes. She responded, *"Con mi dos nalgas, como no."*

In my express desire to impress, I mispronounced the verb *sentir* (which means feel). As a result, instead of asking my grandmother how she was "feeling," I asked her how she "sat"! Of course, she replied "with her two buttocks." This faux pas really provided the family with laughs for months to come. Nani was so humored; she immediately called up all her sons and daughters, from New York to California, to tell them about the "joke." At first, I was mortified. Later on, however, I remember thinking she really was impressed that I tried. From then on, I read the Mexican newspaper to her every night for at least a year. She helped me with the pronunciation of the words. This, in effect, was how I learned Spanish. It was also during these lessons that I learned about Latin roots and how many words in Spanish are similar to their English counterparts. I became fascinated with how language works.

Now as an adult, I find myself yearning to be able to speak more clearly and coherently in both languages. Although I have a master's degree in English, I still feel inadequate in this language. I struggle searching for words that will illustrate what I am feeling. For those of you who know me well, I believe this is where the flying hands come in!

As for Spanish, I have years to go until I will feel comfortable communicating in this language, which is very close to my heart, but so distant from my tongue. The older I get, the more important it is for me to be able to speak and read this language that originally carried a stigma with it.

Whew! There is so much more that I wish to say, but don't know how. I will close for now, but I must admit, this memoir is making me look at some things that I "knew," but never gave voice to. I am finding out that language acquisition is a most intimate possession.

Adios,
Ceci

My language memoir opened up my students' eyes to their teacher. Needless to say, they laughed at the faux pas that I made with my grandmother. Suddenly, I was human! They realized that I, too, make mistakes with language and that today I can laugh about them. We discussed how my experience was similar to theirs, and how it was different. Of course the initial discussion centered on the obvious—my first language was English and theirs was Spanish. But then the discussion moved away from the obvious and centered on issues far more covert. Feelings, pride, need, loyalty, trust—these were all topics the students began to discuss with me. Next, I asked them to write their own language memoir. Below is the memoir that Samuel posted in September 2000.

La Historia de Mi Life

I came to the US of A when I was about 5. I started preschool in Colorado when I was 6. My first weeks of school were the hardest, everyone spoke different, acted different, and I couldn't understand. This made me feel left out, and I wanted to go home just then.

I'm not sure when my first friend came, but he was the only one that spoke the same as me and he too had come from Mexico with his family, to live the American dream. Both of us could talk and play and now I didn't feel a stranger. As the year went by, I learned a few English words and could say "Hi" or "Bye." When I graduated from preschool and got my diploma, my parents were very proud and happy.

I left preschool ready for kindergarten. Armed with my new English, I started the year. My first week I met Mr. Jaramillo, an ESL (English as a Second Language) teacher. He got me and all the Spanish-speaking students in my grade and started to teach us English. Little by little we learned and soon we could say the alphabet and count to 10.

The years went by and as I went through 1, 2, 3, and all the way to 7th grade, Mr. Jaramillo taught me English. By now I could read, speak, and write in English. Now I could communicate with someone in my class or talk to the teacher. When we went to the store I would read the prices, items, and ask where something was for my mom.

That same summer we moved to Arizona, to Huachuca City to be more precise. I said bye to all my childhood friends, that together we played, grew, and learned English with Mr. Jaramillo. I'll never forget what Mr. Jaramillo did for me, he opened the door to a new world. Coming here has been hard and adapting to school and new people hasn't been easy. Now that I have been living here [in Arizona] for 3 years, I have met new friends and learned new things.

My home has stayed the same throughout all these years, we still talk Spanish and stay true to the Mexican tradition. I live in the barrio and most of my friends speak Spanish, down where I live you'll always see someone playing soccer, basketball, or doing some fixing on their cars, most of them bumping to some Spanish music.

I still see myself as a Mexican, just one that has learned to live in the USA and part of a family that is living the American dream.

As I read Samuel's entry, I couldn't help but smile at how he immediately began playing with the language. His title, "La Historia de Mi Life," speaks to the duality of his language experience. This is not only a history of his language acquisition, but a history of his life.

Now, the real work would begin as we all began posting and responding to each other's words. After posting our memoirs, the teacher researchers began to look closely at what our students were writing and what exactly language acquisition might mean to them. Michael Armstrong guided us in reading student work critically, using the same skills and attention we use in the analysis of any literary text. Following Michael's lead, the teacher researcher members adopted the "listening technique" modeled by Carla Rinaldi and Project Zero in the text *Making Learning Visible: Children as Individual and Group Learners* (2001). In this text, Rinaldi states: "Listening is not easy. It requires a deep aware-

ness and at the same time a suspension of our judgments and
above all our prejudices; it requires openness to change" (p. 81).
We all suspended our judgments and read and discussed online
what we saw in the writing. For instance, once Samuel's memoir
was posted, I did not post any historical data on Samuel. All we
had to look at were Samuel's words and what they were saying. The following is an initial impression I wrote of Samuel's
memoir utilizing Rinaldi's technique, which focuses not on what
I think I know, but of what Samuel's writing tells me. So following Rinaldi's lead, I let go of the teacher talk in my head, and I
focused closely on what was in Samuel's narrative, not what was
grammatically correct or not, but what was placed on the page
and how it was placed on the page. My interpretation was then
posted in the Teacher Talk folder for viewing by Mary, Lusanda,
and Michael only:

> As is evidenced by Samuel's narrative, retaining Spanish
> remains crucial to him. Interestingly enough, however,
> the title of his narrative demonstrates how aware he is
> of straddling two worlds. His first four words are all in
> Spanish and then "Life" appears. His understanding of
> the difficulties of learning and utilizing a language are
> clear, yet he remains playful. The acquisition of English
> brought with it added responsibilities and awareness. For
> instance, Samuel mentions how Mr. Jaramillo "opened
> the door to a new world" for him by teaching Samuel to
> read, write, and speak English. In this new world, Samuel
> has been able to meet new friends and interpret for his
> mother, but "it hasn't been easy." Of course, the narrative
> also demonstrates the difficulties he experienced in ob-
> taining a new language while retaining his identity.

Watching the Story Develop

The sharing of our own language stories became the catalyst
that allowed this project to bloom through participant responses and develop into the powerful conference that it has become.
Following is a response to Samuel's memoir that was written

by Khulekani Njokweni, a student at the University of Witwatersrand, in Johannesburg, South Africa:

> Hi
> It is exciting to know one of the most spoken languages in the world isn't it. Well I also studied English as a second language at school.
> What I used to do was to read every English material I lay my eyes on. It was difficult, I admit, because at home we spoke Xhosa, which is my home language. So I had to find a way of learning how to communicate in English. I joined the debates society and there my language skills improved dramatically.
> The only thing I can tell you is stay true to your tradition, don't lose your identity and read, then you are on your way to success.
> Ndiyabulela means thank you
>
> —Khulekani

This short, eloquent entry demonstrates how two young men, half a world away from each other, share a similar story. Although Khulekani lives in South Africa, a country that recognizes 11 national languages, and Samuel is in southeastern Arizona, where English is the only recognized language, they connect on a level that was not available to Samuel in the classroom. Khulekani realizes and supports Samuel's need to "stay true to your tradition."

Powered by this affirmation, Samuel began to bloom in the classroom. In English III Samuel still brought in the newspaper, but more often than not he would willingly participate in the discussion in class. His continued writing with students and teachers online, with the discussion focusing on language acquisition, empowered him to understand and accept his role as a bilingual citizen of the United States of America.

Of course, this understanding did not come easily or without a great deal of discussion, writing, and thinking. In an entry from his senior year, after more than 12 months of participating in this conference, Samuel posted a letter that left me and many others baffled. This letter, written as a response to one of Mary

Guerrero's letters in which she explains her own language frustrations, illustrates how the conference conversations initiated deeper understanding among the respondents.

> Dear Mary,
> I know what you mean when you try to say a word in Spanish, but comes out in English, or when the word your thinking of comes out wrong. The thing that I hate is when your out walking around the store or park you hear people holding a conversation in Spanish but then talk in English for awhile then back in Spanish.
>
> —Samuel

As Samuel's classroom teacher, I immediately felt my hackles rise. Why would a student, who had experienced firsthand the reality of intolerance, be himself so intolerant? What motivated Samuel to react to this "code switching" technique? In the safety of the electronic conference, Mary responded beautifully and carefully to Samuel's entry. Below is her response:

> Dear Samuel,
> I am interested in your thoughts about English and Spanish mixed. I have often wondered about this. In fact in school I have studied Latin American poets who mix languages. I love code switching poems. I'm wondering if you could tell me why you hate to hear people talking in English and Spanish. I think that code switching can be a very interesting topic.
> When I first began to learn Spanish in college, I had a Cuban professor who told my friends and I that talking in two languages together was uneducated. She told the students from places like the Dominican Republic, Puerto Rico and Mexico that they should use one language or the other but never mix. I agreed with her at the time but later I started to question whether that really was the answer.
> Now that I am a teacher and I work with students from DR and PR, I notice that these students love to use the two languages together. Also, since they have grown up hearing both languages, the two languages are together for them. I think that sometimes for certain people, in certain situations,

with certain audiences mixing languages is fine. (The other day I listened to some young poets performing for students in our school, at one point the poet switched into Spanish and the crowd roared with joy.) I'm not saying that students shouldn't learn both languages well but I don't think that speaking both is uneducated. In fact I have friends who have finished college and they love to speak English and Spanish mixed when they have the opportunity.

So what do you think about this, Samuel? How do people feel in your community about using both languages? Do you try to speak only one language when you speak to your family or friends?

—Mary

In this response from Mary, Samuel learned the term *code switching* and when and how people might use it. This exchange opened up a nonthreatening space where a teacher researcher could share her personal experience with a student researcher. In Chapter 4 Diane Waff explains that research communities are vital to the potential of the research being conducted—and for expanding what counts as teacher and students. In this project, each participant extended the knowledge and understanding of the work we were doing. Before beginning a teacher-research project, consider the research community you will be sharing your work with, and ask yourself these questions:

- Who will make up this community?
- When will we meet?
- How will we present our information?

Since our research was contained in an electronic folder, we were able to maintain a virtual conversation that could be easily followed and sustain its momentum.

While Mary's carefully crafted response not only exhibited her academic understanding of language, it also demonstrated her personal understanding of language. Through the space allowed by the electronic conference, Samuel read, processed, and developed his own understanding of language. With this new understanding, Samuel applied the knowledge he gained over the past 18 months as he presented an analysis of one of his favorite songs. He also chose to post this song and his analysis later on in the research folder.

29 Jan 2002

Primer Acto is a song that describes how a person that is born someplace and then grows up in another nation is often looked down on by even his own family or kind. I like it because in a way it relates to all the things that people tell me, like that I'm not a real Mexican or I have turned into a "güerro" and have no real heritage in me. The song goes on to say how the best way to shut them type of critisium is to not pay them any thought and just ignore them. This is very true because sometimes the best words are the ones that can hush.

When someone leaves there home nation to go to another country, looking for a better way of life or a better opportunity for the family, they go to look for a better life. There are some people that always question were your pride or honor for your no longer part of that country. They see you as if you abandoned your home nation. Most of them critiques don't know how hard it is to go outside your country to look for things that your own nation can't offer you. They don't know how it is to live with the fear of never succeeding. No matter were you live, you will always represent your country, your land. The song, "Primer Acto" by the Kumbia Kings, tells all this and the person's feelings in a short, descriptive way that makes the listener stop and think about there home country. That's why I like it and did my song analysis on it.

—Samuel Pacheco

This piece not only reflects Samuel's understanding of the political implications involved in immigration, it also highlights his passion for his homeland. This assignment, which was the analysis of a song and its lyrics and included an oral presentation to the class, really did open my eyes to what Samuel found important in his definition of himself as a bilingual student. First of all, this assignment was a final exam for his English IV class, the third and final class in which I would have Samuel as a student. The fact that he could choose any song and analyze the lyrics for his class demonstrates how important this topic has become to Samuel. Second, that he chose to become vocal about his beliefs, his heritage, and his experience, in a class where he usually remained silent was phenomenal. Needless to say, the class sat silent and enthralled to hear Samuel address them in such an eloquent manner on a topic that obviously meant so much to him. Finally, the work that Samuel had done in the electronic exchange truly came to a sort of fruition here as it allowed him an opportunity to voice what he had been writing to his friends. This breakthrough for Samuel, and for myself as a teacher of second language learners, really underscored the importance of narrative and how our stories can serve as gates into acquiring new language and voices for others to hear.

Bringing It All Together

As part of our research design, we planned a meeting with all the participants. Due to the generous support of the Spencer Foundation, the teacher researchers were able to visit both Tombstone and Lawrence, and in January 2003, everyone—four teacher researchers and nine student researchers—was able to attend a work session in Andover, Massachusetts. For the first time, after more than 2 years of writing to each other online, each participant of the electronic conference was able to meet face to face. Along with our group of original researchers, several other academic researchers joined us for a week of intense discussion centered on language and literacy and what it means to be bilingual (or in South Africa, multilingual). The addition of these academics in language and writing was a natural progression of our online discussion. Through the process of discussing and sharing our language stories, all members of the group established themselves as experts in their own stories. It is important to note here that none of the members of the language acquisition conference felt any imposition by these new members. We had become a solid research community, and not only did we value what we had learned, we invited others to share their knowledge with us. As a matter of fact, we were eager to have outside experts come in and work with us. For that reason, we invited these individuals from across the country to join our conference. This liberating concept allowed for a week of inspired discussion.

Although many of us had never seen each other in real time, we all felt a connection. As a result, when we came face to face, there was little if any discomfort. Even the fourth graders did not hesitate to speak up and address us by our names, and everyone acted and felt as if we had known each other forever. In actuality, this should have been no surprise since we had been sharing our writing and our lives online for so long.

During this work session, we laughed, cried, and rejoiced in the fact that for us the idea of limiting ourselves to one language is absurd. However, we also realized the importance of the work we have been participating in and the political swing that supports "English Only" initiatives and standardized assessment as weapons that will prohibit this very type of research and inquiry process.

Sitting around the table, we went back over the transcripts and asked each other what we may have learned and how, if at all, our ideas about language may have changed. In the course of the discussion, we would break out for guided writing and during one of these writing sessions, fourth grader Jessica wrote about what being bilingual means:

> I think waking up everyday and talking and also thinking in Spanish is pretty neat because if you don't know how to say something in English you can say it in Spanish. But Michael also it's hard because you have to learn how to say things backwards. Let me tell you like you say the white house. But in Spanish you have to say it *la casa blanca*. That means "the house white." So that's hard but it's real hard for me because I have to speak English and then at home I have to speak Spanish. But then I forget and started speaking Spanglish.

This excerpt from Jessica's response demonstrates the liberating effects of this radical research project. Here is Jessica, a fourth grader, directly addressing Michael Armstrong. Neither differences in age nor education prohibited this young student researcher from speaking to her fellow researcher as an equal. Also, in this excerpt, she addresses the difficulties of bilingualism in the United States by using the "white house" as an example. What better symbol of political interference and governmental impact than the home of the president of the United States?

During this work session, Samuel gave the following response to the question, What does it mean to be bilingual?:

> To me, to be bilingual, or to be able to speak two languages fluently, is to have a new door open. It can help you or it can also be the opposite. Maybe, I'm trying to say that sometimes, you can feel embarrassed to speak what you know.
>
> I can speak and write English and Spanish, both with good aptitude. My primary language is Spanish. I am from Mexican decent, and being raised in that type of household taught me to read and write. Trying to find a life full of opportunities, we came to America, and at first we felt odd, a new country and language, were people were different and said things we couldn't understand, that scared me. I bet it will scare anyone, that feeling of insecurity.
>
> Learning to talk English was like learning to walk again. You must start from the bottom and work your way to a level of acceptance by the new world you stepped into. Its hard to explain how the feeling is but its there, your scared to say the wrong word or to be harshly corrected and thus shattering your confidence. The ever constant feeling of the swarm of butterflies that turned to wasps is always there, every time you get ready to talk or to answer a question. To get help from someone is to be lifted up, you have a buddy to help you know, and if you practice it, the language, you get better and better, until you talk 20 a hour and you feel happy you feel accepted. Although sometimes you stutter, or hesitate because you think about the words that have to come out or because you don't want it to come out wrong, you don't say nothing at all. Maybe I trying to say that you get scared, sometimes, when your around people you don't know. We are all governed by this rule, fear. Fear is what moves you to learn something new or improve another. The fear of not being accepted is what moved me to learn English.
>
> After learning English, I saw a whole new world, from a different angle and perspective. It was an open door for you to walk in and a lot of opportunities for you to snag. Now I could make new friends, and count my change, and be

able to go anyplace without getting lost. I could progress at
school better and reach an understanding of social life and
whats accepted. You feel like a little kid with a new toy.

But like everything, new powers come with new unforget-
table problems. Sure you can talk two ways, but your also
faced with the risk of loosing your roots. I am faced with a
problem of language dominance, the language that I talk
most, is the one that I will choose over the other one. English
is what I speak when I go to college, and work, I deal with
it everywhere and know even with my family, I find myself
fighting against my own upbringings and culture conse-
quently.

I feel as if I am forgetting Spanish like if I was ditching my
culture, family, my way of life. Although I still talk in almost
every case in Spanish and listen and read it, I find myself
constantly thinking things in English. Then I tell myself
whats going on here. That's the bad thing about knowing
two or more languages. Your always fighting with which
language to use and when to use it. And around who.

Having said all this, I feel that your culture is who you
are. Languages can change or shape your culture in some
ways. It can even make you forget things that you were
taught by family. I believe the language you speak is the type
of person that you will in the end come out to be. With language you can change your way of life and the way you look
at things, the way you see people around you and how they
will see you.

My biggest problem, well my nemesis, is when people tell
me to stop talking Spanish. I guess that they must feel threat-
ened by a new thing something they have never heard. But if
they could open up there minds and try to learn new things,
they could put that barrier of linguistic shutoff away and
then they could also step into that new world of things and
place just like I have.

*Porque en el fin, el se sale ganando es el que nunca se da por
vencido.*

—Samuel Pacheco

This entry by Samuel, states far more than I, as a teacher researcher, could possibly do by positing my own observations and

findings. Samuel's words not only speak for him, but for the whole project as well. This type of teacher research provides a space for students and teachers to form their own community around issues that are important to them.

LESSONS LEARNED

This final, eloquent admission by Samuel illustrates the myriad ways that language and language acquisition affect second language learners. For them, it is not just a subject to be learned in class. For them, it is not just about reading and writing. For Samuel, and for the members of this electronic research conference, language acquisition is about identity, culture, acceptance, and life. This research project and process has shown me what a gift language is. However, it can also be a weapon to cut and scar. For Samuel—the shy, quiet student in my sophomore class—it was more like "the swarm of butterflies that turned to wasps." Is it any wonder that he kept silent? Now that he is more vocal, at what cost has this voice come? When he writes, "I feel as if I am forgetting Spanish like if I was ditching my culture, family, my way of life," he expresses issues of abandonment that relate directly to his identity. Who will he become if he can only speak English? With whom will he be able to speak? Will he be able to speak to his mother?

As is the case with most teacher research, while many questions have been answered, the questions generated by this project have exceeded the answers we have uncovered thus far. Of his own work with rural children, Leo Tolstoy wrote:

> It's impossible and absurd to teach and educate a child for the simple reason that the child stands closer than I do–and than any grown-up does–to that ideal of harmony, truth, beauty, and goodness to which I, in my pride, wish to raise him. The consciousness of this ideal lies more powerfully in him than in me. All he needs of me is the necessary material to fulfill himself, harmoniously and multifariously. (Blaisdell, 2000, p. 48)

This teacher-research project illustrates that quite well. All that our students needed to fulfill themselves was an opportunity. The electronic conference and the face- to-face conference provided this forum. As an educator in an "English Only" state, which is situated on the border, this conference has truly opened my eyes and my heart to the difficulties of my Spanish-speaking students who come into my classroom searching for a way to quell the wasps and free the butterflies. Samuel's stories, along with the stories of all the researchers, have taught me not only about the power of narrative, but also about the power of sharing our stories.

Participating in this project has allowed me the opportunity to closely look at student writing, share my ideas and my experience with others, and learn from their ideas and experiences. This research project clearly demonstrates the value of utilizing students as coresearchers when learning about issues that they know first hand. Through the collection of information, discussion of writing, and reflection of the experience, my teaching practice has become more informed. Today I know that students bring to the classroom powerful experiences and information that can and should be heard. With this knowledge comes a deep understanding that teacher research not only benefits me, but also my students as we share the space in the classroom.

CHAPTER 4

CORESEARCHING AND COREFLECTING

The Power of Teacher Inquiry Communities

DIANE WAFF

DIXIE GOSWAMI: *In this chapter Diane Waff sends a strong message about the need to support literacy teachers who come together to investigate issues of practice that focus on race, ethnicity, class, and linguistic difference, with the goal of respecting and honoring the cultural and ethnic identities of their colleagues and students. Her research as an African American teacher and administrator in an urban context was influenced by her membership in three different inquiry communities. Diane offers insights into how operating within these spaces helped her develop a critical, reflective stance as a teacher engaged in school reform.*

A thread that runs through Diane's chapter is her experience of learning communities as spaces where teachers cross boundaries of race and role to talk freely about difficult and complex matters, learning from each other. Diane emphasizes the necessity of building collective wisdom in environments that encourage respect for the views of individuals as she demonstrates the connection between membership in successful teacher inquiry communities and supporting student learning in classroom communities. The "web of meaning" that Diane's narrative reveals is that collaborative learning communities are ideal places to engage literacy teachers in urgently needed research that has the potential to influence their own classrooms and, more broadly, the way children are "treated, evaluated, and categorized."

Like Marty and Ceci, Diane demonstrates that teacher researchers should create or find affiliations and networks that give them "safe spaces of real dialogue" to study with others the com-

plex issues of race, class, gender, and language with regard to their "own lives, teaching and learning, and research efforts." While Marty's and Ceci's chapters focus on students as language and literacy learners, Diane's chapter shows us a teacher's perspective of what it is like to teach, learn, and change, and what the experience meant to her and to her colleagues and students. Diane, like Marty and Ceci, is an activist who believes that teacher researchers, within successful inquiry communities, can and do make changes in the lives of teachers and students. Their contributions are important as individual and personal achievements but also as part of a large, dynamic agenda for democratic education that is taking shape in the early years of the twenty-first century in the face of opposing forces.

This chapter explores how my work as a teacher researcher was influenced by participation in three different teacher inquiry communities—a K–12 community focused on multicultural education, a secondary school community focused on teacher leadership, and a K–college community focused on teacher research. Each community provided its own dialogical network that attended as much to the internal resources of its members as it did to academic knowledge and research in the field. Another discourse community emerged as Dixie, Marty, Ceci, and I—all of us connected in one way or another with the Bread Loaf program in writing— prepared this book and worked with the editors of the NCRLL series over a fairly long period of time. We engaged in conversations that ranged from philosophical to rhetorical issues.

While each community had a different purpose, each one helped me to unravel the complexities surrounding my work as an African American teacher and administrator in an urban context. My narrative illustrates how, as a teacher researcher, my sense of meaning about events experienced in classrooms and schools changed as I constructed and reconstructed meaning in the company of colleagues from a range of backgrounds, teaching contexts, teaching levels, and experiences. I examine how my thoughts and actions shifted as I interrogated ideas in the company of colleagues. Moving out from the isolation of the classroom to the shelter of inquiry communities that provided safe spaces for real dialogue, the sharing of stories, relationships with colleagues, and reflection helped me to develop a critical reflective stance with regard to my own teaching and school reform efforts.

TEACHING CONTEXT

My teacher-research narrative begins with my volunteering to coteach a nontracked 11th-grade English class with Suzann, a European American colleague from the Philadelphia Writing Project, in a culturally and ethnically diverse urban high school located in the northeast section of Philadelphia. According to the School District of Philadelphia's Office of Accountability and Assessment's 1999 Disaggregated Data Summary, the Northeast High School population for the year 1998–99 was 60.5% White, 22.5% African American, 8.9% Asian, 7.9% Latino, and 0.3% Native American. The diversity in our classroom community was parallel to the racial and ethnic makeup of the school.

When I began to coteach the class, I was also working full-time as a Teaching and Learning Network (TLN) coordinator with responsibility for designing professional development and providing in-class support to teachers in the Northeast cluster. I taught the class with Suzann from 7:30 to 8:30 each morning before beginning my duties as TLN coordinator. I knew the classroom experience would help me as a district administrator to keep a focus on what's really important—teaching and learning. This partnership also emphasized the important reciprocal role that I, as a new administrator, could play in improving the quality and effectiveness of classroom instruction—"of both absorbing and being absorbed in—the culture of practice" (Lave & Wenger, 1991, p. 95).

While we were coteaching, Suzann and I shared membership in one inquiry community—Seeking Educational Equity and Diversity—which held monthly seminars after school with an emphasis on culturally inclusive school and classroom environments. In addition, I participated in two other inquiry communities: (1) the monthly Philadelphia Writing Project's Study on Urban Learning and Leading (SOULL), held on Saturday mornings and focused on teacher leadership and what is needed in secondary schools to enhance learning environments and student success; and (2) the spring and summer Carnegie retreats for school- and university-based teacher researchers conducting research on practice.

RECOGNIZING A GOVERNING GAZE

Through the opportunity to dialogue about teaching and learning with differently positioned colleagues in our inquiry communities, Suzann and I were able to take a critical look at our
classroom as a community and to take a hard look at our work
together. We worked collaboratively to recognize what Emig
(1983) calls a "governing gaze," our way of seeing and perceiv-
ing reality. We sought to take into account the race and power dynamics that were woven throughout the social and professional
landscape. We were like the phenomenologist Emig describes as
one who "not only acknowledges context but also scrupulously
locates and describes it" (p. 162). We were mindful of the power
of diverse perspectives and saw our knowing expanded by the
multiple ways of knowing represented in our inquiry communities (Roppel, 2002).

Mishler's (1979) summary of Patricia Carini's view of "personal knowledge" underscores how important it was for us to
have a community to interrogate ideas, foster reflections, and offer insights into some of the unobservable factors affecting our relationships and teaching and learning experiences. Mishler sum-
marizes Carini as follows:

> The perspective of the observer is intertwined with the phenom-
> enon which does not have objective characteristics independent of
> the observer's perspective and methods. Further, it contains mul-
> tiple truths, each of which will be revealed by a shift in perspective,
> method, or purpose. Since reality is knowable in an infinite number
> of ways, many equally valid descriptions are possible. The choice
> among them depends on the purposes of the investigator and the
> focus of the investigation. (p. 10)

Considering problems and issues from the multiple perspectives and vantage points offered by community members helped
me reshape my perceptions and often led to knowledge construc-
tions and reconstructions that I might not have made indepen-
dently. As a result, my ongoing dialogues with Suzann were en-
riched by our joint participation in local and national networks
of teachers about what works to advance literacy teaching and
learning.

Suzann and I agreed that we would focus our research on the ways gender, race, and class transacted with literacy instruction in the literature course Literature of Social Vision and Social Change, as part of the district-mandated 11th-grade theme of Finding America. We intentionally set out to create a liberatory classroom environment that would nurture students to become fluent and critically aware readers and writers. We decided to take an inquiry stance on our practice and embrace the concept of the classroom as a place where language, literacy, and power are braided in ways that create a classroom where all students can be successful. We sought to understand what it means to teach and research language and literacy in ways that would help our students become more reflexively aware of their own socially constructed positions and to consider alternative possibilities. By looking closely at how we created such a context, we believed our research would address something that is largely missing from writing-literacy instruction in the urban setting—an insider's view of what it means to encourage diverse students to take critical stances. Through analysis of our team-teaching practices, talking to students and looking closely at student writing, and discourse in the company of colleagues from three different inquiry communities at various points throughout the year, we deepened our knowledge of the literature-response process in two respects:

- How social context and discourse shapes readers' responses
- How links to other contexts or alliances related to social difference influence the stance and practices of students in small- and whole-group contexts (journal, literature/ peer response)

FOCUSING OUR RESEARCH

Through participation in inquiry communities, we looked closely at our own school and classroom practices. We started asking ourselves and each other questions such as these:

- Do we offer students an opportunity to voice their ideas?
- How many varied perspectives do we invite in the classroom, regardless of a student's racial identity or ability?
- What must change in classrooms in order for all students to have the opportunity to learn and achieve at high levels?

Fueled by the conversations in SOULL, I worked with Suzann to construct a classroom community that would invite diverse participation and shift the responsibility for teaching and learning to all learners in the room. Like Marty (see Chapter 2), we sought to create multiple participant structures to provide students with active learning experiences that would not only engage them in articulating and developing their ideas but also push them to question their existing beliefs in light of alternative perspectives. In the course of their work, both Marty and Ceci (see Chapters 2 and 3) noted that when their students worked in collaboration with adults and peers on a learning task, the students were more engaged and had a deeper understanding of the concepts taught. Drawing upon the constructivist stance expressed by Emig (1983), my partner teacher and I determined to construct a classroom community that would provide students with the opportunity to engage new ideas, learn from each other, and create new knowledge as a classroom community.

Henry Giroux (1991) suggested that educators need to develop a "politics and pedagogy around a new language capable of acknowledging the multiple, contradictory, and complex subject positions people occupy within different social, cultural, and economic locations" (p. 235). In particular, he noted that teachers should play a critical role in challenging and sometimes interrupting the inequities experienced on a daily basis by poor and minority students who are denied the opportunity to see their own realities reflected in the literacy classroom.

The failure to provide a curriculum that offers students both "windows into the realities of others and mirrors in order to see their own realities reflected" (Style, 1998, p. 150) can deny some students the opportunity to develop their voices and see themselves as actors in the world. Style argues that teachers must develop pedagogical structures that provide students with the opportunity to use their own experiences, their history, and their culture as a basis for authorship, for telling their story in their own words. As Ceci demonstrates in Chapter 3, giving students the opportunity to share and respond to each other's life stories opens a channel for honest dialogue and fosters reflection. Feedback from peers and teachers to autobiographical writing helps students reshape perceptions, validates their sense of identity, and provides valuable insights they may not discover on their own. Ceci, through the use of memoir writing, was able to deepen her understanding of ESL students grappling with the complexities of "what it means to be bilingual—to live in two worlds."

RESEARCH METHODOLOGY

The research method underpinning our inquiry is grounded in case study methodology. Janet Emig's (1983) classic study, "Composing Processes of Twelfth Graders," drew on a well-established tradition of case study methodology, a tradition reflected later in her essay "Non-Magical Thinking," in which she describes a process by which teachers create knowledge about themselves and their students as writers. In each of the instances I describe in this chapter, Suzann and I established a context-sensitive methodology for gathering and analyzing data after formulating questions and engaging with dialogue intended to clarify and make transparent our own ideological perspectives. Cochran-Smith and Lytle (1993) include teachers' journals and dialogue around teachers' journals as important sources of data and sites for analysis. Observation and reflective journals, recorded conversations, collection of artifacts, and analysis conducted collaboratively are methods that go across the study I describe.

The accounts I share emerged from my daily experiences as an educator who adopted an inquiry stance on practice (Cochran-Smith & Lytle, 1993). In the course of my own work teaming with a White friend and colleague, Suzann, to teach a culturally responsive English course designed to actively engage students in the exploration of themes like equality, justice, power, identity, and culture through literature, we—the instructors—found that we needed support to develop a critical reflective stance with regard to our own teaching and our personal-professional interactions. Central to our successful collaboration was the opportunity to use our varied inquiry-community meetings to reflect on our partnership, identify conflicts, understand the reasons for the problems, and construct alternative ways of thinking and acting. In each inquiry community we worked within the frame of constructivist methodology, which takes as central lived experiences, relationships between the researcher and the researched, and commitment to articulating and transforming experience.

We used qualitative research methods to collect and analyze the work produced by all participants, which included journal writings focused on readings, written responses to journal entries, inquiry-community reflective writing experiences, reflective journals kept by participants, and data collected that was unique to our individual lines of inquiry. My data also included lesson plans, student work, transcripts, audiotapes, video clips of student interactions, and observations and written texts by graduate students who visited our classroom. Analysis of the data included in this chapter includes explorations of the ways that the diversity represented in these varied inquiry communities served as a resource as I began to problematize the assumptions I held about my own experiences both in and outside of the classroom.

Drawing on Teacher Inquiry Communities

Dialoguing and sharing documentation of teaching practice in a community with like-minded others prompted a collective desire to increase our understanding of our daily experiences not as an end in itself, but rather as a stimulus for pursuing change. Our use of the phrase "What's going on here?" and our persistent questioning about how and why things happened helped our work and our thinking evolve over time, each of us learning from the others' experiences. Over time our responses, as well as our understanding of educational issues, problems, and dilemmas, began to change. In the sections that follow, I will describe my experiences in each of the three inquiry communities in which I participated.

Seeking Educational Equity and Diversity

For Suzann and me, the desire to improve our capacity to advance student achievement was a powerful driver for participating in our varied inquiry communities. During the summer of 2001, we decided to form and participate in an inquiry community that brought together teachers from Seeking Educational Equity and Diversity (SEED), a national teacher network focused on equitable curricular and systemic change, and members of the Philadelphia Writing Project, a community that uses inquiry as a key to provide more equitable results for students. As one of the conveners of this joint inquiry community, I knew partnering the two networks would support my colleague and me, as well as other teachers, in developing a critical reflective stance with regard to our own teaching, reform efforts, and equity issues. Themes we explored included the purpose of schooling, the role schools play in producing social stratification, the social construction of identity, gender oppression, and an examination of the ways our own beliefs and practices unwittingly contribute to the failure of our weakest students.

What made the SEED community unique is that the group was comprised of K–12 teachers along with high school seniors. The SEED community was a rich pastiche of racial, ethnic, and cultural diversity. There were approximately two teachers from each of the nine schools in our cluster, with the majority of staff and students coming from the high school. The group consisted of 10 teachers of color, 20 White teachers, and 10 students from diverse backgrounds (Asian, Latino, White, African American). The high school students in the group, drawn from the classes of participating teachers, wrote letters of application pledging to participate fully in all learning experiences. In addition to reading, writing, and discussing issues of equity and diversity, the group engaged in collaborative inquiry and actively constructed an understanding of the themes explored.

Suzann and I were able to use SEED as a resource as we attempted to take the school district's mandated theme of Finding America and use it to help our students pursue the meaning of literacy and power in their own lives. As a way into the theme, we asked our students to wrestle with the central question: Is there an America other than the one you experience or create? My colleague and I were attempting to reshape the traditional curriculum by helping the students in our class draw upon their own knowledge and experience to understand classroom texts.

Traditionally at our high school, F. Scott Fitzgerald's *The Great Gatsby* (1925) provided the lens for studying the pursuit of the "American Dream." Absent from this perspective were the voices of female, African American, and working-class immigrants on life in America. So with the support of colleagues in SEED, we sought to balance the curriculum for gender, race, and class and provide our students with a broader vision of human experience than that provided in the usual isolated presentation of *Gatsby*.

As a result of looking at the diversity in our classroom, we decided to place the *Gatsby* window on American life next to Richard Wright's *Native Son* (1940), Linda Crew's *Children of the River* (1989), Ruthanne Lum McCunn's *Thousand Pieces of Gold* (1981), and the "textbooks" of our students' own lives (McIntosh and Style, 1994). With the help of our inquiry-community colleagues, we also found two writings by Jewish immigrant Anzia Yezierska that fit perfectly into the theme: an essay, "America and I" (1923/1979), and a book, *Bread Givers* (1925).We hoped that the cultural windows provided by these texts would give students opportunities to see America and the pursuit of the American dream from multiple perspectives. Juxtaposing the lives of Daisy, Jordan, and Nick with the circumscribed life of Wright's Bigger Thomas and the horror and injustice of Jewish and American womanhood in the works of Yezierska and Lum McCunn provided students with clues for analyzing a race and class system that privileges some and discriminates against others.

As we participated in SEED, we used inquiry to document our work and to aid in developing new ideas as we designed learning experiences for the students in the course. The adoption of an inquiry stance strengthened our capacity to take bolder, more effective actions in our schools and classrooms. One of the teachers in our inquiry community objected to our use of the *Bread Givers* because of the way Jewish men, particularly the rabbi, were portrayed. Suzann and I wondered if our respective backgrounds as Italian American and African American (our governing gaze) had clouded our view of Jewish men.

Although we didn't agree with our colleague's position, we decided to take her concern as a real, moral issue and critically explore our curricular decisions with the help of the other teachers in the community. After lots of discussion with educators both in and outside of SEED, we decided upon Chaim Potok's *The Chosen* (1967) as a way to balance out the portrayal of the rabbi. Although our conversations were hard and at times messy, I believe that as a community we were building collective wisdom and moral sensitivity as we began to develop new culturally sensitive orientations to teaching and learning.

Project SOULL: Study of Urban Learning and Leading

I joined Project SOULL, a Philadelphia Writing Project inquiry community, right about the time I started to team-teach with Suzann. SOULL was a group composed of female secondary school teacher-leaders, and university graduate students and faculty. Reflective of the writing project's diversity, the group was composed of four White and four African American teachers, three White college faculty members, and graduate research assistants, including one Latina and one African American woman. This community, which focused on teacher leadership, became for me a safe place to share stories about my teaching experiences and my continuing efforts to grow in my relationship with my partner teacher. When I experienced what I perceived as a breakdown in my professional relationship with Suzann, the SOULL community became a place for solving problems, tensions, and difficulties. I related the following story during a SOULL session:

> A few months ago, my cluster of schools had a Communities of Faith conference, and we brought different groups— Muslims, Jews, Baptists. We were in a Jewish synagogue, and I was there with a group of students from my school and Suzann, a teacher I have been team-teaching with all year. We're all sitting around this big table and one of the African American board members was speaking, a Black minister. Suzann was sitting there with the Home and School president who is a rather powerful woman who starts talking to Suzann. They talked the entire time this man was speaking. And I thought, my God, you know, if it were a rabbi, would she talk the whole time? There are students sitting there— there's an African American young woman, two Asian students, and three White kids. This one White boy, after he's looking at the two of them talking, pulls out Tic-Tac-Toe and starts playing.
>
> Suzann and I talk about respect and the need for active listening and hearing different perspectives, and that was the purpose of this Communities of Faith conference, to talk about how we're going to connect with the communi-

ties of faith, how we're going to work with these diverse groups of kids we have in our schools, and how we're going to develop partnerships with people in the community. But then Suzann and the Home and School president are there talking while this man is speaking. And I thought if I say absolutely nothing, then I'm colluding with them. What is the best strategy? And so I leaned over and I looked directly at Suzann. I said, "How can you talk while he is talking? How can you do that?" And I didn't want to embarrass her. But, you know, the kids are looking too. And she looked pretty embarrassed by me raising this question, and I thought well, was there another way? Should I have written a note and have it travel around the table? This was a huge table and I'm sitting on the other side. I just felt like I had to interrupt it. I needed the kids to see that this should not happen and that you have an obligation to say something, that this is just not right.

While the content of this story is outside of the range of what usually gets shared in most educational contexts, I felt safe enough to discuss it within the SOULL community. Through frank open dialogue, the group raised questions about race, identity, and culture, while sharing and responding from their life experiences. I was able in the company of colleagues to imagine alternative ways of responding to the situation and to explore ways of bridging the gap between Suzann and myself. The group's commitment to seeking deeper understanding, also a ground rule in the SEED community, became not only an end in itself but a stimulus for pursuing change. My subsequent dialogue with Suzann resulted in an examination of the consistencies between our values and our actual actions and practices. Both of us came to the conclusion that even a socially conscious teacher, a morally reflective teacher, may also make mistakes. It was through these discussions that the meanings of ideas were explored and the interrelationships between our ideas, behaviors, and the kind of antiracist, multicultural teaching and learning we sought to promote were clarified.

Carnegie Community

I was among the first cohort of educators accepted into the Carnegie Academy for the Scholarship of Teaching (CASTL) for

K–12 teachers and teacher educators in 1999. CASTL provided a venue for teachers to come together as colleagues and carry out investigations into their own teaching. The community consisted of fourteen K–12 teachers, seven of whom were teachers of color, and six White teacher educators. The Carnegie community merged two historically separate communities into one to "legitimate a scholarship of teaching that has a knowledge base that comes neither solely from the research community, nor solely from teacher experience, but rather makes teaching and learning problematic" (Schulman, Lieberman, Hatch, & Lew, 1999; see http://www.tnellen.com/carnegie/2000.html for a virtual photograph of the group).

I made my work with Suzann the focus of my research. As members of the Carnegie community, we went through the processes of formulating research questions, developing methodology, gaining subject consents, collecting data, analyzing and interpreting data, and finally publishing and disseminating our findings. With so much attention paid to student outcomes and products in the K–12 world, I was surprised that the folks at Carnegie were more interested in the process of teaching and of learning than products and outcomes. Employing Shulman's conception of the scholarship of teaching, we were engaged on two distinct levels: what teachers do to support student learning of subject matter, and the public examination and exchange of knowledge about teaching subject matter. We were supported by members of the Carnegie staff as well as our community colleagues to share richly developed portrayals of teaching and learning in our classrooms. We shared classroom artifacts, class handouts, audio- and videotapes of lessons, and board work that was in some cases either photographed or recorded in field notes and shared. To supplement or expand on the work presented, we participated in a variety of reflective discussions or panel presentations facilitated by the Carnegie staff, some of which were audiotaped or filmed.

The K–12 CASTL gallery (http://gallery.carnegiefoundation. org/gallery_of_tl/castl_k12.html), supported with funds from the Carnegie Foundation for the Advancement of Teaching (CFAT), was designed to give teachers a public and published platform using multimedia to make their work accessible to a variety of audiences. Lee Shulman, CFAT president, asserts that teachers should not only research their practice but also make their work public so that others can critically examine and build on their work and ideas (Hutchings, 1998; Shulman, 2001; Shulman, Lieberman, Hatch, & Lew, 1999). The gallery gives members of the educational community an opportunity to view online the varied work of teacher researchers. Through the pioneering work of Carnegie's Knowledge Media Lab, this technology is now available to teachers across the country who are interested in documenting and sharing their work online. For more information about this easy to learn and use resource, visit http://www.cfkeep.org/static/index.html.

The Carnegie inquiry community sessions forced us as presenters to become metacognitively aware of our teaching methods and made our tacit knowledge explicit and available to members of the community. This process made us voice what was going on in our teaching context and why. Furthermore, it made explicit the principles behind the planning of the unit or lesson presented and gave the audience an opportunity to share an external perspective on "what happened." One of the first questions my colleagues asked me was "Why did you choose the literature you did for the Finding America theme?" I knew there were many other titles that would have supported my students' exploration of the essential question: Is there an America other than the one you experience or create? However unlike my university colleagues, my partner teacher and I did not have a budget to select texts that would have provided a more cohesive collection for students to explore differing experiences of American society. We were limited to the books in the book closet. The challenge Suzann and I faced was how to help our students develop a critical reflective stance about American society using the canonical texts we had on hand.

The teachers in the Carnegie community, more through example than collaborative lesson planning, helped me to discover how to make productive use of the people and material resources that were in my school and classroom. Emily Style refers to this as using a combination of "selves and shelves" (quoted in McIntosh, 2007, p. 2) drawing upon the textbooks of our lives as well as the books on the classroom shelves as a resource. I learned to appreciate, as well as productively mine, the treasures in the room when diverse teachers, students, cultures, discourses, and ideologies meet in a classroom.

Using the context of a teacher-research piece written by a well-known teacher researcher, we explored the complexities of power and representation in teacher research, and what it means for a teacher to report research without taking into careful consideration the benefit to the student who is the object of that research. Issues of ethics, equity, race, and morality bubbled to the surface as we discussed a White teacher researcher's portrayal of a Black at-risk youngster. One African American teacher asked, "Why did the teacher lay bare so many intimate details of the child's life?" Another asked, "How did the student benefit from being in the teacher's classroom much less from being the subject of her research?" The entire community was taken aback by the intellectual bite of these teachers' queries. I must admit that on my first read of the piece I too had concerns, but I did not feel comfortable articulating my views in a community that I thought held up this teacher researcher's work as an exemplar. The perspectives of the two African American teachers were hotly contested as we struggled as a community to find some common ground. At first, the group divided largely along racial lines as we debated the relationship between the teacher and her student. As we talked, we moved from discussing that particular piece of research and began to question the moral dimensions of our own research and pedagogic judgments. We raised the following questions:

- What are the moral obligations of a teacher's work who conducts research while shaping the learning and lives of her or his students?
- What are the components necessary for a scholarship of teaching and learning?

Shulman (2002) writes,

> The scholarship of teaching and learning rests, that is, on a moral claim that I will call the "pedagogic imperative." We argue that an educator can teach with integrity only if the effort is made to examine the impact of his or her work on the students. The "pedagogical imperative" includes the obligation to inquire into the consequences of one's work with students. This is an obligation that devolves on individual faculty members, on programs, on institutions, and even disciplinary committees. (p. viii)

Our dialogues about pedagogic actions and ethical research, responsibility to the students versus responsibility to the research, encouraged teachers across race and teaching position to freely express their opinions and to use the inquiry community as a context for learning from each other. With the building of collective wisdom came eyes more attentive to the needs of the students and new images of classroom communities in which all members are free to express their opinions and are responsible for appreciating and respecting the views of their colleagues.

Connecting Teacher Inquiry Communities and Classroom Communities

Marian Mohr and her K–12 teacher-research colleagues write that there is a unique symmetry between teacher inquiry communities and the classroom communities of its members:

> Teacher researchers working with colleagues create a learning community within a school that affects student learning, professional development, and school decision making. This community develops because of changes in the way teacher researchers view themselves and others and through the identification of the contexts in which they work together. (Mohr, Rogers, Sanford, Nocerino, & Clawson, 2004, p.17)

As an inquiry-community member, I learned that if differences are silenced in the interest of congenial relations, then meaningful dialogue leading to either changes in perspective or the consideration of alternate perspectives is precluded (DuFour, 2003). Because my understanding of the practices necessary to build and sustain a collaborative learning community for teachers deepened, my beliefs about the practices needed to support student learning in a classroom community changed. The social practices used by the National Writing Project (NWP) to cultivate community, which are identified by Anne Lieberman and Diane Wood (2003) in their research of NWP sites, embodies my understanding of what makes teacher inquiry communities successful. They list ten practices:

- Approaching each colleague as a potentially valuable contributor
- Honoring teacher knowledge
- Creating public forums for teacher sharing, dialogue, and critique
- Turning ownership of learning over to learners

- Situating human learning in practice and relationships
- Providing multiple entry points into the learning community
- Guiding reflection on teaching through reflection on learning
- Sharing leadership
- Promoting a stance of inquiry
- Encouraging a reconceptualization of professional identity and linking it to professional community (p. 22)

While outlined as practices that support professional learning communities, the lines for me between communities for teacher learning and student learning are blurred. Suzann and I worked collaboratively to put these practices in place in our classroom to ensure that our students felt valued, were free to express their opinions, and were responsible for respecting and appreciating the views of others.

Transmissive instructional techniques were jettisoned in favor of constructivist teaching strategies and representations of subject matter. Amanda Branscombe (1987) describes such a pedagogical shift as the ability to see teaching as a "learning pilgrimage or search" with the students. She became a colearner and coexplorer with her students because the rigid level of hierarchy between teacher and student was removed. Similarly, Vanessa Brown (2005), a special education teacher in Philadelphia, built a classroom community based upon her conviction that students are nurtured as learners when we create environments that genuinely engage students in conceptualizing problems and addressing them as a collective body. The trick, according to both Brown and Branscombe, is not merely to change our teaching practices but to help our students discover and build on their strengths as communities with the power to open up new vistas and provide varied lines of inquiry. Brown suggests that we contribute to the scholarship of teaching by "disrupting the discourse that supports the status quo of trapping children in preset boundaries" (p. 265).

In our classroom the literature-circle dialogues, the journal group discussions, and the guided reading inquiry experiences gave our students an opportunity to share alternate perspectives and to consider their ideas in relationship to others. As the discussion of the ideas presented in the course texts deepened through class discussion, dramatic enactments, and reflective essays, the events described in the books became less abstract as students began to relate the issues in the text to those in their own lives as well as in the broader society. Students began to question the existence of a universal experience of America. The America the pilgrims found was not necessarily the America experienced by Asian, African, or Jewish immigrants.

As part of our teaching strategies, Suzann and I showed films like *Hester Street* (Silver & Silver, 1975) and *Yentl* (De Waay, Lemorande, & Streisand, 1983) and also displayed some of the portraits of the 75 African American women from a range of social class backgrounds who are pictured in Brian Lanker's photo essay *I Dream A World* (1999). Drawing upon a learning experience developed by Emily Style, we asked students in their reading of *The Great Gatsby* to imagine the responses of one of the women profiled in Lanker's book to the statement that Fitzgerald has his character Daisy Buchanan make: "the best thing a girl can be in this world is a little fool." The assignment provoked student thinking about gender bias and class privilege in interesting ways. We taught Gatsby in a unit rich with women and people of color enlivened by students sharing from what McIntosh and Style (1994) refer to as the "textbooks of their lives" (p. 126).

To collect data for our research, we videotaped classroom sessions, audiotaped small- and whole-group conversations, wrote field notes of each class session, analyzed transcripts, looked closely at student writing, and talked daily about what we were learning from our data. We retained copies of our lesson plans and made copies of the graphic organizers generated during our discussion of literature texts. The graphic organizers generated during the class analysis of Crew's *Children of the River* (1989) give a sense of the intense conversations during the pre- and postdiscussions of an excerpt from the book. You can see a sample of the map and other aspects of our work on the Web site Suzann and I developed with the support of Carnegie at http://gallery.carnegiefoundation.org/collections/castl_k12/dwaff/index.html/.

The students brought unique vantages to the ways in which people are constrained and shaped by their sociocultural environments and the courage it takes to make decisions that cut across the grain. My partner and I took the opportunity to echo Rosenblatt (1965) in pointing out the danger in the unquestioning adoption of positions that many of us have been socialized to take. Rosenblatt writes, "Literature invokes participation into the experience of others and comprehension of their goals and experiences" (p. 88). The students were able to reflect as a community on the conflicts that arose when they, like the characters in the texts they read, attempted to go against the advice of parents and grandparents in their choice of friends, music, clothing, and so on. The cognitive and emotional support the students gave and received from each other developed strong bonds within the group, built their confidence as learners, and created a classroom community that in many ways mirrored the professional inquiry communities described in this chapter. Bransford (1994) writes that reading the text as a community enables students to question preexisting schemata and to begin to construct new schemata (p. 487). In making various intertextual links (book texts and life texts), students really became oriented to the problems the characters faced.

The identification of stereotypes in the *Children of the River* was a painful experience for many Asian students in the class, and it opened the eyes of peers to the insidious nature of stereotypes and the way they influence how you read and understand a text. As students began to unpack some of the images of Asians presented in the text, it became what Langer (1995) terms an "envisionment building" experience (p. 38). Rosenblatt (1965) refers to this as "evoking the novel." The students began to read the text in different ways, often through the eyes of differently positioned classmates.

The concept of American as normal and foreign as strange was a powerful macro-idea that enabled the students to look critically at the images of Americans and Asians presented in the text and to hear and understand multiple perspectives. Bransford (1994) writes that "introducing students to relatively sophisticated core concepts can provide a basis for understanding the significance of a variety of new facts" (p. 494). The linking of everything normal with American, as reflected in the character of fair, open-minded, "blue-eyed" Jonathan versus the portrayal of the "yellow peril" (student quote) Pok Simo as the revengeful, class-conscious Asian opened heated conversation about the images in the air about various cultural groups and gendered identities. Many White male students in the class felt their classmates were going overboard in picking out the stereotypes in the story. I cautioned that the classroom is the place for critical sharing of all perspectives. I really felt that we were beginning to disrupt the traditional balance of power in the classroom by creating safe spaces for students to question how their subjectivities as raced, classed, and gendered beings get produced and lived out on a day-to-day basis both within and outside of the classroom.

Student resistance to stereotypes of passive Asian women and spiteful, scorned American women deepened, as students were able to exchange ideas and critically analyze their own conceptions of gender and racial images operating in the text and in their own experiences. Through grappling with the conflicts and tensions between opposing points of view in the classroom, students were able to recognize that their own beliefs and attitudes were influenced by the images afloat in the world. This insight further deepened student understanding of how difficult it is for people who do not fit the broader society's notion of what it is to assimilate. Biculturalism as the ability to comfortably integrate American culture and the culture of their ancestors became an exciting notion for many. Our students, like my Carnegie community colleagues, developed the awareness that examining the question "What's going on here?" from diverse perspectives is essential to developing a critical reflective stance with regard to their own lives, as well as teaching and learning and research efforts.

IMPORTANCE OF TEACHER RESEARCH

There is a clear and immediate need for insight into the ways social issues transact with the literacy classroom and for teachers to become reflective scholars and researchers of teaching. Several factors make this insight imperative. One factor is the changing demographics. Suzann and I began the design and implementation of our course Literature of Social Vision and Social Change with the goal of working with the students in our diverse classroom to develop a critical consciousness while acquiring high-level literacy skills. As we developed and carried out this course, we were continually assessing what our students were gaining from the experience, including shifts that were occurring for them in their concepts of themselves as learners and critical thinkers. At the same time, we were looking closely at the pedagogical strategies we were using to apprehend and build upon our students' diverse backgrounds and experiences. We were simultaneously researchers and objective observers as we continuously listened to and shared classroom data with members of our varied inquiry communities.

As we worked with inquiry-community colleagues, our thinking about the classroom context and the content of instruction surrounding and leading to students' taking a critical inquiry stance evolved. We found that, to be effective, we had to create a social context for literacy learning in the classroom that encouraged students to look at the constitutive nature of discourse, to take on the social construction of their own identities, to imagine alternative ways of being, to consider consequences, and to learn by doing. Creating the conditions at the classroom level that we enjoyed in our teacher inquiry communities provided students with rich opportunities for peer group dialogue that gave them access to new ways of seeing, new ways of responding to literature, and, in many cases, new ways of seeing themselves.

Taking an inquiry stance propelled students into expressing their own points of view and raising questions. The complexities of students' lives surfaced as they shared their writing, and the collective experiences of the group became the data we pulled from in addressing issues raised in the texts or in understanding classroom interactions and perspectives. For the students in our class, the course served as an apprenticeship to academic discourse and critique. Like their teachers, they came to understand how to look beyond their individual environment, experience, and knowledge and use the diverse backgrounds and experiences in the classroom and beyond as resources.

Suzann and I were able to transform our classroom practice by integrating the inquiry-driven, collaborative practices we experienced in our varied teacher-inquiry communities into our classroom. The resulting pedagogical shift generated a change in the way we thought about curriculum decisions and teaching, our interactions with students, and the social dynamic in the classroom. I have found that teachers who participate in supportive inquiry communities like SEED, SOULL, and CASTL succeed in making complex changes in their practice. The opportunity to share inquiries based on individual teaching contexts and to learn from each other's experiences generates new knowledge that helps teachers make a difference in improving student learning.

CHAPTER 5

RESOURCES FOR DOING YOUR OWN
TEACHER RESEARCH

MARTY RUTHERFORD
CECI LEWIS

This book is about teacher inquiry. Though different in content and context, the shared purpose that binds these examples of teacher research (in fact, all teacher research) together is that teachers do research in their classrooms because we care about our students and want to do the very best we can for them. Systematically and carefully executed research builds relevant local knowledge about our particular students. This is important because local knowledge—knowledge about the very unique students who populate our classroom—is essential for building learning environments that are responsive to their very specialized needs. Teacher researchers have a unique view into classroom teaching and learning because we are on the inside (Cochran-Smith & Lytle, 1993).

The constant that runs through all teachers' inquiry is that through this kind of careful observation we learn and build knowledge about what it means to educate and liberate students so that they can think, read, write, and speak about their own worlds, the worlds they inhabit. This is urgent work for every teacher. As the celebrated theorist and teacher Louise Rosenblatt (2005) wrote just before she died at the age of 100:

> I have constantly been energized by the tacit belief that language energizes the whole person and can enable us to reach beyond our-selves as we make the choices that compose our lives. To jump out

of the way of an oncoming car—life as against death—is easy. In settled times, most choices can be made just as automatically, according to values absorbed from family, peer group, the media, school, or community. In our tumultuous, changing world, beset by poverty, pollution, and war, unthinking, ready-made responses are dangerous. Sometimes we must choose between alternative positive values, such as security and freedom of speech. How much should we give up of one or the other, in order to have both? There must be a weighing of priorities. (p. x)

As teachers, that is our work, to build classrooms where our students acquire the tools that they need to engage in this "weighing of priorities." Our challenge is to know when we are meeting this goal and when we are not. Teacher research is the single most powerful tool for seeing, really seeing, our own practice and the impact, intended or otherwise, that it is having on our students.

This book allowed for entry into our worlds of teaching, including the lives of our students, their parents, and our colleagues. Our gaze was always impacted by our desire to be better teachers, plain and simple.

The three examples represented in this book are just that: three examples. In the genre of teacher inquiry there is no single way of looking. The classroom is too complex. Close observation of young people in the process of learning requires a carefully and uniquely constructed system of inquiry. One with checks and balances to make sure the looking and learning is true to the context and our students.

Because there is no such thing as one-size-fits-all in teacher research, what follows is an annotated bibliography with resources that have assisted each of us in our inquiries. This is meant as a starting place. In conducting the research represented in this book, we clearly drew on the invaluable resources of our students, fellow teachers, and colleagues to build our understanding. We also had help from "published friends." These people were teacher and university-based researchers who made their work available for wider consumption. Sometimes this resource was available in books, other times on line, at conferences, or through local universities. What follows is a list of helpful friends. This list is by no means exhaustive; it is just a starting point for your own research.

Now that we are in the time of the Internet, finding sources is relatively simple. Finding good and reliable information is a completely different matter. When looking for resources to inform your own practice or inquiry it is helpful to have a starting point. Use the people represented in this chapter as one link in a chain of work that covers a range of experiences and information. Look to their work as a bridge to your own if it is useful.

On the most practical level, when we engage in our own research, one of the very best first practices is to look at the bibliography of a book or article that is particularly rigorous, helpful, and informative. As you already value the research of the person(s) you are reading, it is a good bet that what they read to inform their own work will be helpful to you and your research. Finally, the bibliography in this book is comprised of the people who helped us understand the research represented in this book. Each person represented is well worth consideration should his or her work be relevant to your work.

As a way to facilitate the usefulness of the following annotated bibliography, we have divided the sections into the following categories: Learning the Basics; Published Teacher Research; Building Theories; and Supportive Institutions.

LEARNING THE BASICS

The books in this section have supported our practice over the years. As with every section in this chapter, this list is partial, but a good start.

Cochran-Smith, M., & Lytle, S. (Eds.) (1993). *Inside/outside: Teacher research and knowledge.* New York: Teachers College Press.

> A number of well-established academics have a long and wonderful history exploring, valuing, and championing teacher research and teachers who do this work. At the top of the list are Marilyn Cochran-Smith and Susan Lytle. Their steadfast commitment to make the work of teachers engaging in inquiry part of the ongoing dialogue about how children learn is long and tireless. It includes being editors of one the first series of published books (see Teachers College Press), holding numerous conferences for teachers, as well as hosting the renowned teacher research section of the Penn Ethnography conference for over 20 years—the list goes on and on. We recommend all of their work. One of the earliest collections about teacher research that includes actual teacher research is this volume. It presents a clear de-

scription of the value of knowledge built and then made public from the inside out.

Dyson, A., & Genishi, C. (2005). *On the case.* New York: Teachers College Press.

This is a wonderful step-by-step guide about how to conduct a case study. Dyson and Genishi, deeply experienced case study researchers, teach us what it means to be "On the Case" by walking through two actual cases. Along the way, we learn about forming research questions, collecting data, and writing it up. Unlike the Hubbard and Powers books (see below), this book has a very explicit focus on linguistic minority students. Additionally, there is much to be learned in this book about how to build theoretical frames for understanding our own research.

On the Case is part of a larger series of volumes in the NCRLL collection. The editors of this series, Donna Alvermann and JoBeth Allen, explain that the NCRLL series *Approaches to Language and Literacy Research* offers "definitive information and guidance in using different research approaches in the field of language and literacy education" (p. vii). This series is particularly helpful for teachers engaging in research. As we have repeatedly stated, there is no one size fits all. Nor is there one genre of research that will meet all your needs in your inquiry projects. The NCRLL *Approaches to Language and Literacy Research* collection provides great how-to assistance across research paradigms.

Emig, J. (1983). *The web of meaning: Essays on writing, teaching, learning and thinking.* Upper Montclair, NJ: Boynton/Cook.

Even though the authors of the current volume have been engaging in teacher research for almost 2 decades, revisiting this seminal work provided new insights and guidance. Though we have done our best to faithfully present Emig's inquiry framework, there is nothing as fine as going to the original source.

Goswami, D., & Stillman, P. (Eds.) (1987). *Reclaiming the classroom: Teacher research as an agency for change.* Upper Montclair, NJ: Boynton/Cook.

For all the authors of the current volume (save Goswami), *Reclaiming the Classroom* was their starting point—an invitation into the world of teacher research. This book lays the groundwork for why teacher research is urgent, important, and necessary. Dividing the book into four parts, the editors of this book, along with the authors of each chapter, help the reader gain a deeper understanding of why classroom inquiry is important, how it serves as an agency for change, and how to plan for research, concluding with a collection of teachers' research that punctuate each of the aforementioned sections. The authors of this book are our "elders." They were builders of the genre that became our tradition. It is quite simply a must-read.

Himley, M., & Carini, P. F. (Eds.) (2000). *From another angle: Children's strengths and school standards.* New York: Teachers College Press.

This book represents the work of scores of teachers with a connection to the Prospect School, which is world renowned not only for great teacher inquiry but also for powerful documentation of practices. In this book, founding members of the Prospect School describe the Descriptive Review Process. Simply put, the Descriptive Review Process is a multifaceted way of looking at our students within a school context. Although largely considered an oral process, it can easily be adapted to be an incredible source of data for a written inquiry project. The process is a carefully articulated protocol for understanding the relationship of the student as a person and the implemented curriculum. This is just one book published by this amazing group of researchers. Every thing they do is worth a close and careful read.

Hubbard, R. S., & Powers, B. M. (1993). *The art of classroom inquiry: A handbook for teacher researchers.* Portsmouth, NH: Heinemann.

Hubbard and Powers explain the process of turning thoughts or hypotheses into research. Beginning with the basics of research strategies, the authors present interviewing and note-taking techniques, methods for characterizing data, and avenues for publishing research.

Hubbard, R. S., & Powers, B. M. (1999). *Living the question: A guide for teacher researchers.* Portland, ME: Stenhouse.

This book is an old tried and true friend. It literally takes you from your first moment of thinking about engaging in teacher research to finding a question, methodology, analysis, and the all-important step of writing it up. The authors set the stage for conducting research by using actual teachers' research. They explore issues such as the value added from doing research; how to develop and evolve research questions into plans; collecting and analyzing data; reading others to inform practice; and the challenge of writing up the research.

A limitation of this book is the lack of inclusion of ample resources that deal with teaching and learning in diverse learning communities. For example, there is not nearly enough on issues surrounding bilingualism. However, its strength is that it is practical and straightforward. This book does not have to be read from cover to cover to be useful. You can pick and choose the parts that are most useful to you. In our busy lives, this is a big plus!

Published Teacher Research

Happily, more publishing companies now feature work by teachers engaging in research than when we all began this work. Teachers College Press has a whole series on Practitioner Research. Heinemann has long been a supporter of teachers' work. Stenhouse is another notable publisher. A growing number of publishers—both online and paper—are displaying a growing interest in this field.

Armstrong, M. (2006). *Children writing stories.* Maidenhead, UK: Open University Press.

> It is possible that Michael Armstrong is one of the most magical teachers ever born. Much of his teaching now takes place at the Bread Loaf School of English teaching teachers and at conferences populated by young people. His ways of looking closely at children's work is so utterly captivating that once Michael finishes the explanation of how to look at writing, a flurry of youngsters' hands from 5 to 18 years of age fly into the air and a chorus of voices cry out, "Do mine, Michael, do mine!" Virtually every student and teacher present wants to learn the wondrous process described in elegant detail in this book. Read, devour, and enjoy.

Ballenger, C. (1998). *Teaching other people's children: Literacy and learning in a bilingual classroom.* New York: Teachers College Press.

> The value of teacher researchers working with the support of strong inquiry communities is visible in this story of a White teacher who drew upon the support of colleagues both in and outside of school to grapple with and understand the sociocultural problems she encountered working with Haitian American students in her preschool classroom. Interrogating classroom discourse as well as her own deeply held beliefs and assumptions with inquiry-community colleagues helped Ballenger diminish the cultural barriers to teaching her students well.

Benson, C., & Christian, S. (with Goswami, D., & Gooch, W.) (Eds.) (2002). *Writing to make a difference: Classroom projects for community change.* New York: Teachers College Press.

> Separated into three distinct parts—Writing for the Community, Writing for a Networked Electronic Community, and Writing for Change— this book provides examples of successful writing projects that place students at the center of teaching and learning in each classroom represented and at the center of each teacher's research.

This book is a wonderful resource for generating ideas for our own classrooms and communities. The teachers and students featured in each chapter provide excellent examples of what can occur when teachers and students work together to write for change. The chapters demonstrate what works and what doesn't when it comes to developing these writing communities. Whether the change in writing is curricular as in "Creating a Writing Community through Drama," or the change is in social responsibility as displayed in "Rural Communities, Gangs, and School Violence: Writing for a Local and Electronic Community," the essays in this text demonstrate how writing for change can occur in classrooms. The layout of the text allows for easy accessibility to the reader's preferred avenue of research and development.

Fecho, B. (2003). *"Is this English?" Race, language, and culture in the classroom.* New York: Teachers College Press.

A meticulous teacher researcher, Fecho carefully guides us through a careful exploration of his high school classroom. In so doing, we begin to see firsthand the complexity of the intersection between race, language, and culture in the classroom. The well-represented voices of his students allow for the building of deep knowledge about teaching and learning. This book is a wonderful model for doing teacher research. Fecho is generous and open in sharing his process and practice. It is impossible to put this book down once you enter into the classroom of these and amazing and powerful students from Philadelphia.

Freedman, S. W., Kalnin, J. S., Casareno, A., & the M-Class teams. (1999). *Inside city schools: Investigating literacy in multicultural classrooms.* New York: Teachers College Press.

This is an essential read if you are teaching in a multicultural classroom wondering about ways to provide robust literacy experiences for your kids. The work represented in this book is the result of a collaborative study among 24 public school teachers from Chicago, Boston, New Orleans, and the San Francisco Bay Area and four university professors from National Center for the Study of Writing and Literacy at the University of California in Berkeley.

The purpose of the Multicultural Collaborative for Literacy and Secondary Schools (the M-CLASS Project) was to allow the teachers to find effective ways to explore their practice and transform their findings into usable knowledge for other teachers in similar classroom settings. The result is a collection of studies that are gritty, honest, and immensely helpful both in terms of gaining ideas for teaching and for acquiring essential tools for conducting your own research. While the heart of the book is the teachers' descriptions of their own experiences of dealing with race, class, and gender issues in their classroom, the discussion of the implications of this kind of research conducted by the university partners is very illuminating.

Obidah, J., & Teel, K. M. (2001). *Because of the kids: Facing racial and cultural differences in urban schools.* New York: Teachers College Press.

For anyone who is interested in race, teaching, and learning, this is a must-read work. Obidah, a Black teacher, and Teel, a White teacher, engage in a cross-racial and cross-cultural collaboration to help Teel improve her effectiveness in teaching students of African descent. Obidah and Teel address difficult questions surrounding race and whiteness in this surprisingly honest and revealing account of their work together in Teel's middle school classroom over a 3-year period. This study serves as a powerful learning tool for educators interested in transforming schools and classrooms into places where all students, regardless of background, have a chance to learn and achieve.

Paley, V. G. (1981). *Wally's stories: Conversations in the kindergarten.* Cambridge, MA: Harvard University Press.

This text, which has many wonderful firsthand accounts of student discussions in the kindergarten classroom, is not only incredibly readable and enjoyable but also powerful in the way that it addresses the myriad roles a teacher encompasses. Paley provides thoughtful reflection of her teacher research process and provides an excellent example of the "aha" moments that teacher research provides. One of the most important aspects of this text is how Paley recognizes the "near misses" she would have lost had it not been for her active research. All classrooms are rich, multilayered environments and Paley's text demonstrates the importance of capturing these layers.

While *Wally's Stories* is our favorite, each and every work by Vivian Paley is absolutely extraordinary and well worth the read and the learning experience. Some of her most poignant work is being done now that she has retired from the classroom and is looking back over her long and amazing career.

Building Theories

Anzaldúa, Gloria (1987). *Borderlands/la frontera: The new mestiza.* San Francisco: Aunt Lute Books.

Insightful and inciting, this book demands that the reader position himself or herself somewhere in the reading experience. Anzaldúa does not offer easy access to the reader. While this may create an uncomfortable situation for the reader, it does demand that the reader acknowledge the writer and the situation. The introduction and first chapter are especially well worth the effort as they clearly show the reality of border life. As Anzaldúa illustrates, every person's experience is different, and it serves us well to understand that our students share in this uniqueness. Although frustrating at times, this text is important because it provides historical, linguistic, and political explanations for the experiences of people who live in a border culture.

Bruner, J. (1986). *Actual minds, possible worlds.* Cambridge, MA: Harvard University Press.

Since Bruner is considered one of the leading thinkers about how children learn, it is worthwhile to spend some time reading his books. Though the wording is difficult and very "academic," it is well worth the effort to plow through some of the chapters in this volume. For the authors of this book, Bruner's work on the language of education, modes of thinking, and Vygotsky were particularly helpful.

Cazden, C. (2001). *Classroom discourse: The language of teaching and learning.* Portsmouth, NH: Boynton/Cook.

For teachers interested in the impact of language on teaching and learning, this is arguably the finest book written on the subject. Each chapter in this book is couched in wonderful examples drawn directly from the classroom with a host of essential supporting theories as to why one action was perhaps preferable over another. A premier theorist about how children learn through language in the classroom setting, Cazden always keeps the teacher in mind as her audience while describing the complex phenomena.

The book includes informative and useful discussions about the central issues facing teachers and students as they strive to become sense makers though their classroom experience. Topics include the value of classroom talk and learning, the role of traditional and nontraditional lessons, classroom discourse and student learning, peer talk (including face-to-face and online); and differential treatment and cultural differences.

Cazden, a Harvard professor emeritus and Bread Loaf faculty, is a longtime valued mentor to each of the authors of this book. She has contributed in enumerable and powerful ways to our understanding of teaching and learning. We wholeheartedly recommend all of her work to help build understanding about how diverse student populations learn in school.

Reyes, M., & Halcon, J. J. (Eds). (2001). *The best for our children: Critical perspectives on literacy for Latino learners.* New York: Teachers College Press.

This fine volume is one of the few collections that include literacy research about Latino children by Latino scholars. As such, it provides important and valuable insights into the diverse learning assets and needs of Latino youth. This book is divided into three sections: The first section explores the sociocultural, sociohistorical, and sociopolitical literacy context as it relates to school, the classroom, and learning for Latino children—the fastest growing demographic in the United States. The second section examines biliteracy, hybridity, and other literacies; it is about what Reyes calls "unleashing possibilities" (Reyes, p. 96). The final section of the book is about empowering kids through language by examining issues surrounding literacy strategies that support and enhance learning.

Heath, S. B. (1983). *Ways with words: Life, language, and work in communities and classrooms.* Cambridge, UK: Cambridge University Press.

More than 2 decades ago this seminal work charged us to attend to two urgent issues: (1) being very careful with words and meaning making, and (2) carefully documenting our practice so that we really know the power of language and how it is used in our classrooms. These issues are still front and center in what each of us as teachers should consider and do on a daily basis.

The book looks at two communities of more or less equal economic status and two different races. Heath careful unpacks how the children in these communities make sense out of school based on their home language and experience. The two communities speak different varieties of English yet the way the children understand and interpret school is very different. In an elegantly executed work, Heath shows us, up close and personal, how these differences are learning assets. Moreover, she makes a compelling argument that only through careful documentation of our own teaching can we first surface the differences in learning and language that exist in our classrooms so that we, too, can use the differences as invaluable resources.

Moffett, J. (1981). *Active voice: A writing program across the curriculum.* Upper Montclair, NJ: Boynton/Cook.

When first published in the early 1980s, this book made a major impact on all those who were teaching English. The book presented a curriculum with innovative ideas that, for a while, became commonplace in high schools across the country. Moffett proposed practices such as workshops, the process approach, writing portfolios, and writing across the curriculum. *Active Voice* takes the reader through a precisely explained, theory-based, sequenced curriculum that creates optimal conditions for all students to become strong communicators in writing. Specifically, Moffett explores writing processes associated with prewriting, midwriting and postwriting activities. Moffett's program is a powerful set of sequenced activities that include exercises to move inner speech to text, composing dialogues and monologues and moving from narrative into essay. The accompanying explanation of these interconnected exercises creates a powerful theoretical framework for the teaching of writing.

Valdés, G. (2001). *Learning and not learning English: Latino students in American schools.* New York: Teachers College Press.

Through three very poignant and comprehensive case studies, Valdés gives us a close-up and personal experience of being a middle school bilingual student. This book clearly demonstrates why so many of our students are and are not learning English in the classroom setting. Along the way she teaches the reader what it means to be bilingual and explains the literacy demands placed on students who are in the process of learning English and the ways we, as classroom teachers, can provide support. Through the amazing and often painful multiyear study about three bilingual middle school students; Valdés explains what access to English in a school setting entails, including the benefits of a well-designed and supportive curriculum versus the potential for failure when attention is not given to the needs of the language learner. She concludes with an in-depth discussion about implications for policy and practice, effective schooling for immigrant students, the politics of teaching English, and an examination of critical pedagogy in English as a Second Language. This book, like everything Valdés writes, is straightforward, to the point, and right on target about the essential issues concerning the education of linguistic minority students.

Vygotsky, L.S. (1978). *Mind in society: The development of higher psychological processes.* Cambridge, MA: Harvard University Press.

By now Vygotsky's "zone of proximal development" is a well-publicized concept, often mentioned in articles and books about how young people learn. While many have done a fine job explaining Vygotsky, there is nothing like going to the source. And once there, you will find a lot more than an explanation of the ZPD. Vygotsky was a powerful theorizer. His work on play, imagination, and creativity has never been more urgent to read and understand. His argument as to the importance of play to intellectual development is compelling. His work on the role of curriculum and learning is clear and essential. He quite simply is a genius, and it is always worthwhile to visit such folks from time to time.

SUPPORTIVE INSTITUTIONS

A number of wonderful institutions supported teacher research over the years. The trouble with any list, however, is what is *not* on the list. The following examples are meant as a start, to help the thinking process about what is locally available. More information is available online for each to the institutions mentioned.

The Bread Loaf School of English has been not only a founder but also a long-standing supporter of teachers engaging in research. Bread Loaf is the home of the longest running, technology-supported professional network. Literally on a daily basis, teachers around the world are developing and sharing their inquiries online with their colleagues. Ceci Lewis's chapter is one example of the fine work done by teachers in this network.

Many universities now have master's programs that are built around teachers doing inquiry. Check out the university near you. They may be able to give valuable support and resources to your work.

The longest running conference that supports teacher research is the Annual Ethnography in Education Research Forum at the University of Pennsylvania Graduate School of Education. Apart from the obvious dedication to ethnographic research, for more than 20 years this conference has opened its doors to teachers as a place to present their research, thoughts, and knowledge about what it means to teach and learn in this time. This wonderfully supportive environment is a great place for all teacher researchers, no matter their experience level, to engage in and present their ongoing inquiries. It is equally valuable as a place to hear other people's work and network with teachers across the country and around the world.

The National Writing Project (NWP) and all of the local writing projects have been strong and unwavering supporters of teacher inquiry for decades. Either go to the NWP Web page (http://www.nwp.org) or find your local group and see what they are doing.

The National Council of Teachers of English (NCTE) not only gives money to teachers who are interested in doing research, they also encourage teachers to present their work at their national conferences. This is a great resource for publishing work and for finding the work of other teachers.

The American Education Research Association (AERA) has an annual conference. Within the conference there is a special interest group created and supported by teachers who do research. This conference is a wonderful place to connect with teachers across the country and around the world that share an interest in this kind of research.

Concluding Thoughts

It is best to end as we began, with the words of Dixie Goswami. When asked by anyone about teacher inquiry, she always responds with the same words, "Just do it." That is the deal; just do it. Nothing will give you a better, more comprehensive window into your practice and into what ways kids are learning—or not learning. Moreover, each student serves as a powerful archetype for others who will follow. Over the years you will build invaluable knowledge about how young people learn.

And then there is the part about responsibility. As teachers, we are so privileged each day to see how kids learn. Our knowledge is from the inside. That unique perspective must continue to enter, with more regularity, into mainstream conversations about education. We must share—share what it means for kids to learn to write, communicate, read for understanding, think, imagine, invent, create, to be bilingual, to be multilingual.

It is time to bring these stories, revelations, and knowledge about how young people learn to a wider audience. The good news is that systematic inquiry, when well conceived and conducted, has the power to illuminate and inform practice. The better news is that it is even more powerful when we engage in this practice as coresearchers with our students. It is our ardent hope that this book inspires you to do just that.

References

Anzaldúa, G. (1987). *Borderlands/La frontera: the new mestiza*. San Francisco: Aunt Lute Books.

Armstrong, M. (1999, June). *The origin of narratives and the narratives of origin* [Class notes]. Ripton, VT.

Armstrong, M. (2006). *Children writing stories*. Maindenhead, UK: Open University Press.

Ash, D. (1995). *From emergent biology to deep biological principles*. Unpublished manuscript. University of California, Berkeley.

Baetens-Beardsmore, H. (1986). Definitions and typologies. In *Bilingualism, basic principles* (2nd ed.) (pp. 1–41). Clevendon, England: Multilingual Matters.

Ballenger, C. (1999). *Teaching other people's children: Literacy and learning in a bilingual classroom*. New York: Teachers College Press.

Benson, C., & Christian, S. (with Goswami, D., & Gooch, W.) (Eds.) (2002). *Writing to make a difference: Classroom projects for community change*. New York: Teachers College Press.

Blaisdell, B. E. (2000). *Tolstoy as teacher*. New York: Teachers and Writers Collaborative.

Bogdan, R. C., & Biklen, S. K. (1982). *Qualitative research for education: An introduction to theory and methods*. Boston: Allyn & Bacon.

Branscombe, A. (1987). I gave my classroom away. In D. Goswami & P. Stillman (Eds.), *Reclaiming the classroom: Teacher research as an agency for change* (pp. 206–218). Upper Montclair, NJ: Boynton/Cook.

Branscombe, A., Goswami, D., & Schwartz, J. (1992). *Students teaching, teachers learning*. Portsmouth, NH: Boynton/Cook.

Bransford, J. (1994). Schema activation and schema acquisition: Comments on Richard C. Anderson's remarks. In R. Rudell, M. Rudell, & H. Singer (Eds.), *Theoretical models and processes of reading* (pp. 483–495). Newark, DE: International Reading Association.

Britton, J. (1987) *Writing and reading in the classroom* (Technical Report No. 8). Berkeley: University of California, Center for the Study of Writing.

Brookline Teacher Research Seminar (BTRS). (2003). *Regarding children's words: Teacher research on language and literacy.* New York: Teachers College Press.

Brown, A. L. (1994) The advancement of learning. *Educational Researcher, 23*(8), 4–12

Brown, A. L., Ash, D., Rutherford, M., Nakagawa, K., Gordon, A., Campione, J. (1993). Distributed expertise in the classroom. In G. Salomon(Ed.), *Distributed Cognitions* (pp. 188–225). Cambridge: Cambridge University Press.

Brown, A. L., Bransford, J. D., Ferrara, R. A., & Campione, J. C. (1983). Learning, remembering and understanding. In J. H. Flavell & E. M. Markman (Eds.), *Handbook of child psychology: Vol.3. Cognitive development* (4th ed.) (pp. 515–529). New York: Wiley.

Brown, A. L., & Campione, J. C. (1994). Guided discovery in a community of learners. In K. McGilly (Ed.), *Classroom lessons: Integrating cognitive theory and classroom practice* (pp. 229–270). Cambridge, MA: MIT Press.

Brown, V. (2005). Human agency, social action, and classroom practices. In T. Hatch, D. Ahmed, A. Lieberman, D. Faigenbaum, M. Eiler White, & D. Pointer Mace (Eds.), *Going public with our teaching: An anthology of practice* (pp. 257–266). New York: Teachers College Press.

Bruner, J. (1986). *Actual minds, possible worlds.* Cambridge, MA: Harvard University Press.

Cazden, C. (1999). The language of American students in classroom discourse. In C. T. Adger, D. Christian, & O. Taylor (Eds.), *Making the connection: Language and academic achievement among African American students in classroom discourse* (pp. 31–53). McHenry, IL: Delta Systems; and and Washington, DC: Center for Applied Linguistics.

Cazden, C. (2001). *Classroom discourse: The language of teaching and learning.* Portsmouth, NH: Boynton/Cook.

Cervone, B. (2006). Student research for action: Restoring hope where it's all but gone. *National Civic Review, 95*(1), 23–25.

Cochran-Smith, M. & Lytle, S. L. (1993). *Inside/outside: Teacher research and knowledge.* New York: Teachers College Press.

Cochran-Smith, M. & Lytle, S. L. (1999). Relationships of knowledge and practice: Teacher learning in communities. *Review of Research in Education, 24*, 249–305.

Crew, L. (1989). *Children of the river.* New York: Bantam-Doubleday.

Cummins, J. (1981). Age on arrival and immigrant second language learning in Canada: A reassessment. *Applied Linguistics, 2*, 132–149.

De Waay, L., Lemorande, R., & Streisand, B. (Producers), & Streisand, B. (Director). (1983). *Yentl* (Motion Picture). United States: MGM/UA Entertainment.

DuFour, R. (2003, Summer). Leading edge: Collaboration lite puts student achievement on a starvation diet. *Journal of Staff Development, 24*(3), 1–5.

Dyson, A. H. (1989). *Multiple worlds of child writers: Friends learning to write.* New York: Teachers College Press.

Dyson, A. H. (1993). *Social worlds of children learning to write in an urban primary school*. New York: Teachers College Press.

Dyson, A. H., & Genishi, C. (2004). *On the case: Approaches to language and literacy research*. New York: Teachers College Press.

Edelsky, C. (1989). Bilingual children's writing: Fact and fiction. In D. M. Johnson & D. H. Roen (Eds.), *Richness in writing: Empowering ESL students* (pp. 165–176). New York: Longman.

Ellis, R. (1985). Teacher-pupil interaction in second language development. In S. Gass & C. Madden, (Eds.), *Input in second language acquisition* (pp. 69–86). Rowley, MA: Newberry House.

Emig, J. (1983). *The web of meaning: Essays on writing, teaching, learning, and thinking*. Upper Montclair, NJ: Boynton/Cook.

Ervin-Tripp, S. (1974). Is second language learning like the first? *TESOL Quarterly, 8*(2), 111–127.

Fecho, B. (2004). *"Is this English?": Race, language, and culture in the classroom*. New York: Teachers College Press.

Fillmore, L. W. (1979). Individual differences in second language learning. In C. J. Fillmore, W. S. Y. Wang, & D. K. Kempler (Eds.), *Individual differences in language ability and language behavior* (pp. 203–228). New York: Academic Press.

Fillmore, L. W. (1991). Second language learning in children: A model of language learning in social context. In E. Bialystok (Ed.), *Language processing by bilingual children* (pp 49–69). Cambridge: Cambridge University Press.

Fillmore, L. W. (1992). Learning a language from learners. In C. Kramsch & S. McConnell-Ginet (Eds.), *Text and context: Cross-disciplinary perspectives on language study* (pp. 46–66). Lexington, MA: D. C. Heath.

Fitzgerald, F. S. (1925). *The great Gatsby*. New York: Scribners.

Freedman, S. W., Kalnin, J. S., Casareno, A. & The M-Class teams. (1999). *Inside city schools: Investigating literacy in multicultural classrooms*. New York: Teachers College Press.

Geertz, C. (1983). *Local knowledge: Further essays in interpretive anthropology*. New York: Basic Books.

Giroux, H. (1991). *Border crossings: Cultural workers and the politics of education*. New York: Routledge.

Giudici, C., Rinaldi, C., & Krechevsky, M. (Eds.) (2001). *Bilingual education and the second language acquisition theory*. Cambridge, MA: Harvard Graduate School of Education.

Goodman, S. (2003). *Teaching youth media: A critical guide to literacy, video production, and social change*. New York: Teachers College Press.

Goswami, D. & Stillman, P. (Eds.) (1987). *Reclaiming the classroom: Teacher research as an agency for change*. Upper Montclair, NJ: Boynton/Cook.

Grosjean, F. (1982). *Life with two languages: An introduction to bilingualism*. Cambridge, MA: Harvard University Press.

Heath, S. B. (1983). *Ways with words: Life, language, and work in communities and classrooms*. Cambridge: Cambridge University Press.

Heath, S. B. (1999). *ArtShow: Youth and community development.* Washington, DC: Partners for Livable Communities.

Himley, M., & Carini, P. F. (Eds.). (2000). *From another angle: Children's strengths and school standards: The Prospect Center's descriptive review of the child.* New York: Teachers College Press.

hooks, b. (1994). *Teaching to transgress: Education as the Practice of Freedom.* New York: Routledge.

Hubbard, R., & Power, B. (1998). *The art of classroom inquiry.* Portsmouth, NH: Heinemann.

Hutchings, P. (Ed.). (1998). *The course portfolio: How faculty can examine their teaching to advance practice and improve student learning.* Washington, DC: American Association for Higher Education.

Krashen, S. (1982). Bilingual education and the second language acquisition theory. In California State Department of Education, *Schooling and the language minority students: A theoretical framework* (pp. 51–77). Sacramento: California State Department of Education.

Kuhn, T. S. (1970). *The structure of scientific revolutions.* Chicago: Chicago University Press.

Lanker, B. (1999). *I dream a world.* New York: Stewart, Tabori & Chang.

Langer, J. (1995). *Envisioning literature: Literacy understanding and literature instruction.* New York: Teachers College Press.

Lave, J., & Wenger, E. (1991). *Situated Learning: Legitimate peripheral participation.* Cambridge: Cambridge University Press.

Lieberman, A., & Wood, D. (2003). *Inside the National Writing Project: Connecting network learning and classroom teaching.* New York: Teachers College Press.

Lindfors, J. W. (1987). *Children's language and learning. Englewood Cliffs.* NJ: Prentice-Hall.

Lum McCunn, R. (1981). *Thousand pieces of gold.* Boston: Beacon Press

Lytle, S. L. (2006). The literacies of teaching urban adolescents in these times. In D. Alvermann, K. Hinchman, D. Moore, S. Phelps, & D. Waff (Eds), *Reconceptualizing the literacies in adolescents' lives* (2nd ed., pp. 279–296). Mahwah, NJ: Lawrence Erlbaum.

McIntosh, P. & Style, E. (1994). Faculty-centered faculty development. In P.F. Bassett & L.M. Crosier (Eds.), *Looking ahead: Independent school issues and answers* (pp. 125–131). Washington, DC: Avocus.

McIntosh, P. (2007). Foreword. In I. Towery, R. Oliveri, & C. Gidney (Eds.), *Peer-led professional development for equity and diversity: A report for teachers and administrators based on findings from the SEED Project (Seeking Educational Equity and Diversity)* (pp. 1–2). Cambridge, MA: Schott Foundation for Public Education.

McKay, S. L. (1989). Topic development and written discourse accent. In D. M. Johnson & D. H. Roen (Eds.), *Richness in writing: Empowering ESL students* (pp. 253–262). New York: Longman.

Mishler, E. (1979, February). Meaning in context: Is there any other kind? *Harvard Education Review, 49,* 1–19.

Moffett, J. (1981). *Active voice: A writing program across the curriculum.* Upper Montclair, NJ: Boynton/Cook.

Moffett, J., & Wagner, B. J. (1983). *Student-centered language arts and reading, K–13: A handbook for teachers* (3rd ed.) Boston: Houghton Mifflin.

Mohr, M., Rogers, C., Sanford, B., Nocerino, M. A., & Clawson, S. (2004). *Teacher research for better schools.* New York: Teachers College Press.

Mohan, B. A. (1986). *Language and content.* Reading, MA: Addison-Wesley.

Murnane, R. J., & Levy, F. (1996). *Teaching the new basic skills.* New York: Free Press.

Obidah, J. E., & Teel, K. M. (2001). *Because of the kids: Facing racial and cultural differences in school.* New York: Teachers College Press.

Paley, V. G. (1981). *Wally's stories: Conversations in the kindergarten.* Cambridge: Harvard University Press.

Paley, V. (1986). On listening to what children say. *Harvard Educational Review, 56,* 122–131.

Palincsar, A. S., & Brown, A. L. (1984). Reciprocal teaching of comprehension-fostering and monitoring activities. *Cognition and Instruction, 1*(2), 117–175.

Potok, C. (1967). *The chosen.* Greenwich, Connecticut: Fawcett.

Project Zero and Reggio Children. (2001). *Making learning visible: Children as individual and group learners.* Project Zero and Reggio Children. Cambridge: Harvard Graduate School of Education.

Reyes, M. (1992). Challenging venerable assumptions: Literacy instruction for linguistically different students. *Harvard Educational Review, 62*(4), 427–445.

Reyes, M. & Halcon, J. J., (Eds). (2001). *The best for our children: Critical perspectives on literacy for Latino learners.* New York: Teachers College Press.

Rogoff, B. (1994). Developing understanindg of the idea of communities of learners. *Mind, Culture, and Activity, 1* (4).

Romaine, S. (1984). The acquisition of literacy and its role in communicative competence. In B. Blackwell (Ed.), *Literacy, the language of children and adolescents: The acquisition of communicative competence* (pp. 92–11). London: Oxford University Press.

Roppel, R. (2002). Rural communities, gangs, and school violence: Writing for a local and an electronic community. In C. Benson, S. Christian, D. Goswami, & W. Gooch (Eds.), *Writing to make a difference: Classroom projects for community change* (pp. 105–123). New York, Teachers College Press.

Rosenblatt, L. (1965). *Literature as exploration.* New York: Modern Language Association.

Rosenblatt, L. (2005). *Making meaning with texts.* Portsmouth, NH: Heinemann.

Royster, J. J. (2000). *Traces of a stream: Literacy and social change among African American women.* Pittsburgh: University of Pittsburgh Press.

Rutherford, M. (1995). *We can't fight with our fists, words are our power: Children in the middle school years learning to write academic prose.* Unpublished doctoral dissertation. University of California, Berkeley.

Shulman, L. (2001). The scholarship of teaching and learning, a perspective after four years. Report of the president from the 96th annual report. Stanford, CA: Carnegie Foundation for the Advancement of Teaching.

Shulman, L. (2002). Foreword. In P. Hutchings (Ed.), *Ethics of inquiry: Issues in the scholarship of teaching and learning* (pp. v–viii). Menlo Park, CA: The Carnegie Foundation for the Advancement of Teaching.

Shulman, L., Lieberman, A., Hatch, T., & Lew, M. (1999, Winter). Research on teaching and teacher education in the 21st century: The Carnegie Foundation builds the scholarship of teaching with K–12 teachers and teacher educators. *AERA, Teacher and Teacher Education, Division K Newsletter.*

Silver, R. (Producer), & Silver, J. (Director). (1975). *Hester Street* (Motion Picture). United States: Home Vision

Strachan, W., & Zoukis, E. (1992). Savoir our connaitre? Alternative ways of knowing in the foreign language class. In Branscombe, A., Goswami, D., & Schwartz, J. (Eds.), *Students teaching, teachers learning* (pp. 46–62). Portsmouth, NH: Boynton/Cook.

Style, E. (1998). Curriculum as window and mirror. In C. Nelson & K. Wilson (Eds.), *Seeding the process of multicultural education* (pp. 149–156). Plymouth, Minnesota: Minnesota Inclusiveness Program

Swain, M. (1985). Communicative competence: Some roles of comprehensible input and comprehensible output in its development. In S. Gass & C. Madden (Eds.), *Input in second language* (pp. 235–256). Rowley, MA: Newberry House.

Tannen, D. (1989). *Talking voices: Repetition, dialogue, and imagery in conversational discourse.* New York: Cambridge University Press.

Valdés, G. (1992). Bilingual minorities and language issues in writing: Toward profession-wide responses to a new challenge. *Written Communication, 9,* 85–136.

Valdés, G. (2001). *Learning and not learning English: Latino students in American schools.* New York: Teachers College Press.

Valdés-Fallis, G. (1978). Code switching in the classroom. *Language in Education: Theory and practice, 4,* 6–26.

Villanueva, V. (1993). *Bootstraps: From an American academic of color.* Urbana, IL: National Council of Teachers of English.

Vygotsky, L. S. (1978). *Mind in society: The development of higher psychological processes.* Cambridge, MA: Harvard University Press.

Walker, J. (1998). Struggles with the dynamics of grouping. In J. Shulman, R. Lotan, & J. Whitcomb (Eds.), *Group work in diverse classrooms: A casebook for educators* (pp. 39–44). New York: Teachers College Press.

Wright, R. (1940). *Native son.* New York: Harper Collins

Yezierska, A. (1925). *Bread givers.* New York: Persea Books.

Yezierska, A. (1979). *America and I.* In A. Kessler-Harris (Ed.), *The open age: An Anzia Yezierska collection* (pp. 20–32). New York: Persea Books. (Original work published 1923)

INDEX

About the Authors

Dixie Goswami teaches at the Bread Loaf School of English at Middlebury College (http://www.middlebury.edu/academics/blse/), where she codirects the Bread Loaf Teacher Network. Dixie directs Write to Change, a nonprofit that promotes writing, digital media, and social change (http://www.strom.clemson.edu/teams/literacy/write.html). After teaching professional writing for many years at Clemson University, she is a senior scholar at Clemson's Strom Thurmond Institute (http://www.strom.clemson.edu). She spends a lot of time on BreadNet, with friends, mentors, young people, and others, but has time for her many great-grandchildren.

Ceci Lewis spent the past 13 years teaching high school English in rural southeastern Arizona. As a secondary education instructor, she has participated in several networks, which help to sustain her work and energy. Some of the networks include the Bread Loaf Teacher Network, National Council of Teachers of English, Arizona English Association, Arizona Education Association, and National Education Association. As a classroom teacher, Ceci has linked her classroom with classrooms across the country and world. Her students have had the opportunity to network with students in other states, including New Mexico, South Carolina, Alaska, Ohio, Maine; Nairobi, Kenya; and Johannesburg, South Africa. These electronic exchanges have all utilized BreadNet and have been made possible through support and funding from the Bread Loaf Teacher Network, the Spencer Foundation, and the National Endowment for the Humanities. Currrently, Ceci teaches English at Cochise Community College and continues working with diverse teacher networks that include Bread Loaf Teacher

Network, Andover/Bread Loaf, New Orleans's Students at the Center, and Write to Change.

Marty Rutherford, after completing her doctoral work in language and literacy at the University of California–Berkeley, went to work at the Spencer Foundation to be part of a team that launched an initiative to provide funds for teachers wishing to build their capacity to engage in research. Both Dixie Goswami and Diane Waff were part of the original board for this grant program. Ceci Lewis's research was funded through this program. After leaving Spencer, Rutherford spent the next several years working on a national, federally funded research initiative called the High Performance Learning Community (HPLC) project. The purpose of this grant was to work with low-performing, high-poverty schools across the country. The HPLC project provided the opportunity for Rutherford to spend 3 years working with nine Yup'ik village schools in Alaska. Once again the focus was on understanding issues of language and literacy through systematic inquiries into how local conditions and context impact teaching and learning. Currently, Rutherford is Director of Curriculum and Development at the Center for the Art of Translation in San Francisco and teaches at University of California–Davis in the teaching credential program. The focus of this program is teacher research, which is used as a vehicle for learning.

Diane Waff teaches at the University of Pennsylvania in the Graduate School of Education. Prior to joining the Penn faculty, Diane spent 3 years as a senior program associate at WestEd in Oakland, California. She has extensive experience as a high school teacher, district and building administrator, K–12 teaching and learning coordinator, and teacher researcher. For more than 2 decades she has worked with teacher research communities as a convener and facilitator for the National Writing Project, the Bread Loaf Teacher Network, and Seeking Educational Equity and Diversity. She serves on the board of the Practitioner Initiated Inquiry Series for Teachers College Press and was the chair of the National Council of Teachers of English Secondary Section Steering Committee from 2006–2008.